THE UPPER CASCADES AT LINVILLE FALLS, PISGAH NATIONAL FOREST

AUTUMN COLORS ON THE RIDGES NEAR THE TENNESSEE BORDER

A SEDGE-COVERED PEAT BOG IN MONONGAHELA NATIONAL FOREST

MIST ON THE RUSSELL FORK RIVER AT THE VIRGINIA-KENTUCKY BORDER

SNOW-DUSTED PEAKS AT SUNSET IN WESTERN NORTH CAROLINA

EARLY SPRING IN CHEAT RIVER CANYON, WEST VIRGINIA

A SILVERY FLUTTER OF WIND-BLOWN SILVER-BELL AND TULIP TREES IN THE SMOKIES

Other Publications:

THE GOOD COOK
THE SEAFARERS
THE ENCYCLOPEDIA OF COLLECTIBLES
THE GREAT CITIES
WORLD WAR II
HOME REPAIR AND IMPROVEMENT
THE WORLD'S WILD PLACES
THE TIME-LIFE LIBRARY OF BOATING
HUMAN BEHAVIOR
THE ART OF SEWING
THE OLD WEST
THE EMERGENCE OF MAN
THE TIME-LIFE ENCYCLOPEDIA OF GARDENING
LIFE LIBRARY OF PHOTOGRAPHY
THIS FABULOUS CENTURY
FOODS OF THE WORLD
TIME-LIFE LIBRARY OF AMERICA
TIME-LIFE LIBRARY OF ART
GREAT AGES OF MAN
LIFE SCIENCE LIBRARY
THE LIFE HISTORY OF THE UNITED STATES
TIME READING PROGRAM
LIFE NATURE LIBRARY
LIFE WORLD LIBRARY
FAMILY LIBRARY:
  HOW THINGS WORK IN YOUR HOME
  THE TIME-LIFE BOOK OF THE FAMILY CAR
  THE TIME-LIFE FAMILY LEGAL GUIDE
  THE TIME-LIFE BOOK OF FAMILY FINANCE

THE SOUTHERN APPALACHIANS

THE AMERICAN WILDERNESS/TIME-LIFE BOOKS/ALEXANDRIA, VIRGINIA

BY JEROME DOOLITTLE
AND THE EDITORS OF TIME-LIFE BOOKS

Time-Life Books Inc.
is a wholly owned subsidiary of
TIME INCORPORATED

FOUNDER: Henry R. Luce 1898-1967

Editor-in-Chief: Hedley Donovan
Chairman of the Board: Andrew Heiskell
President: James R. Shepley
Vice Chairmen: Roy E. Larsen, Arthur Temple
Corporate Editors: Ralph Graves, Henry Anatole Grunwald

TIME-LIFE BOOKS INC.
MANAGING EDITOR: Jerry Korn
Executive Editor: David Maness
Assistant Managing Editors: Dale M. Brown, Martin Mann, John Paul Porter
Art Director: Tom Suzuki
Chief of Research: David L. Harrison
Director of Photography: Robert G. Mason
Planning Director: Thomas Flaherty (acting)
Senior Text Editor: Diana Hirsh
Assistant Art Director: Arnold C. Holeywell
Assistant Chief of Research: Carolyn L. Sackett
Assistant Director of Photography: Dolores A. Littles

CHAIRMAN: Joan D. Manley
President: John D. McSweeney
Executive Vice Presidents: Carl G. Jaeger, John Steven Maxwell, David J. Walsh
Vice Presidents: Peter G. Barnes (Comptroller), Nicholas Benton (Public Relations), John L. Canova (Sales), Nicholas J. C. Ingleton (Asia), James L. Mercer (Europe/South Pacific), Herbert Sorkin (Production), Paul R. Stewart (Promotion)
Personnel Director: Beatrice T. Dobie
Consumer Affairs Director: Carol Flaumenhaft

THE AMERICAN WILDERNESS
Editorial Staff for *The Southern Appalachians*:
Editor: Robert Morton
Text Editors: Marion Buhagiar, Rosalind Stubenberg, Johanna Zacharias
Picture Editor: Patricia Hunt
Designer: Charles Mikolaycak
Staff Writer: Carol Clingan
Chief Researcher: Martha T. Goolrick
Researchers: Lea G. Gordon, Reese Hassig, Trish Kiesewetter, Howard Lambert, Ellie McGrath, Editha Yango
Design Assistant: Vincent Lewis

EDITORIAL PRODUCTION
Production Editor: Douglas B. Graham
Operations Manager: Gennaro C. Esposito
Assistant Production Editor: Feliciano Madrid
Quality Control: Robert L. Young (director), James J. Cox (assistant), Michael G. Wight (associate)
Art Coordinator: Anne B. Landry
Copy Staff: Susan B. Galloway (chief), Susan Tribich, Florence Keith, Celia Beattie
Picture Department: Joan Lynch
Traffic: Jeanne Potter

CORRESPONDENTS: Elisabeth Kraemer (Bonn); Margot Hapgood, Dorothy Bacon (London); Susan Jonas, Lucy T. Voulgaris (New York); Maria Vincenza Aloisi, Josephine du Brusle (Paris); Ann Natanson (Rome). Valuable assistance was also provided by: Carolyn T. Chubet, Miriam Hsia (New York).

The Author: Jerome Doolittle spent his youth in the foothills of Virginia's Blue Ridge and revisited the area in the course of writing this book. He worked as a reporter, columnist and assistant city editor for *The Washington Post* and subsequently, in the 1960s, as a press attaché for the United States Information Agency. Mr. Doolittle has contributed articles to a number of national publications, including *Esquire* and *Holiday*, and wrote *Canyons and Mesas* in this series. He presently lives in Connecticut.

The Cover: The mists of a May morning lend a blue-green cast to the rolling ridges of the Alleghenies, westernmost portion of the Southern Appalachians.

© 1975 Time-Life Books Inc. All rights reserved. No part of this book may be reproduced in any form or by any electronic or mechanical means, including information storage and retrieval devices or systems, without prior written permission from the publisher, except that brief passages may be quoted for reviews.
Second printing. Revised 1979.
Published simultaneously in Canada.
Library of Congress catalogue card number 75-27179.

Contents

1/ Mountains of Subtle Majesty 20
A Lush Botanical Mosaic 38
2/ An Ancient Mantle 54
A Nature Walk in Linville Gorge 72
3/ The Forest Floor 86
Shy Giants of the Hills 104
4/ The Living Water 116
The Raw Beauty of a Wild River 134
5/ Echoes from the Ice Age 146
Winter Moods in the Smokies 166

Bibliography 180
Acknowledgments and Credits 181
Index 182

Mountains of Understated Beauty

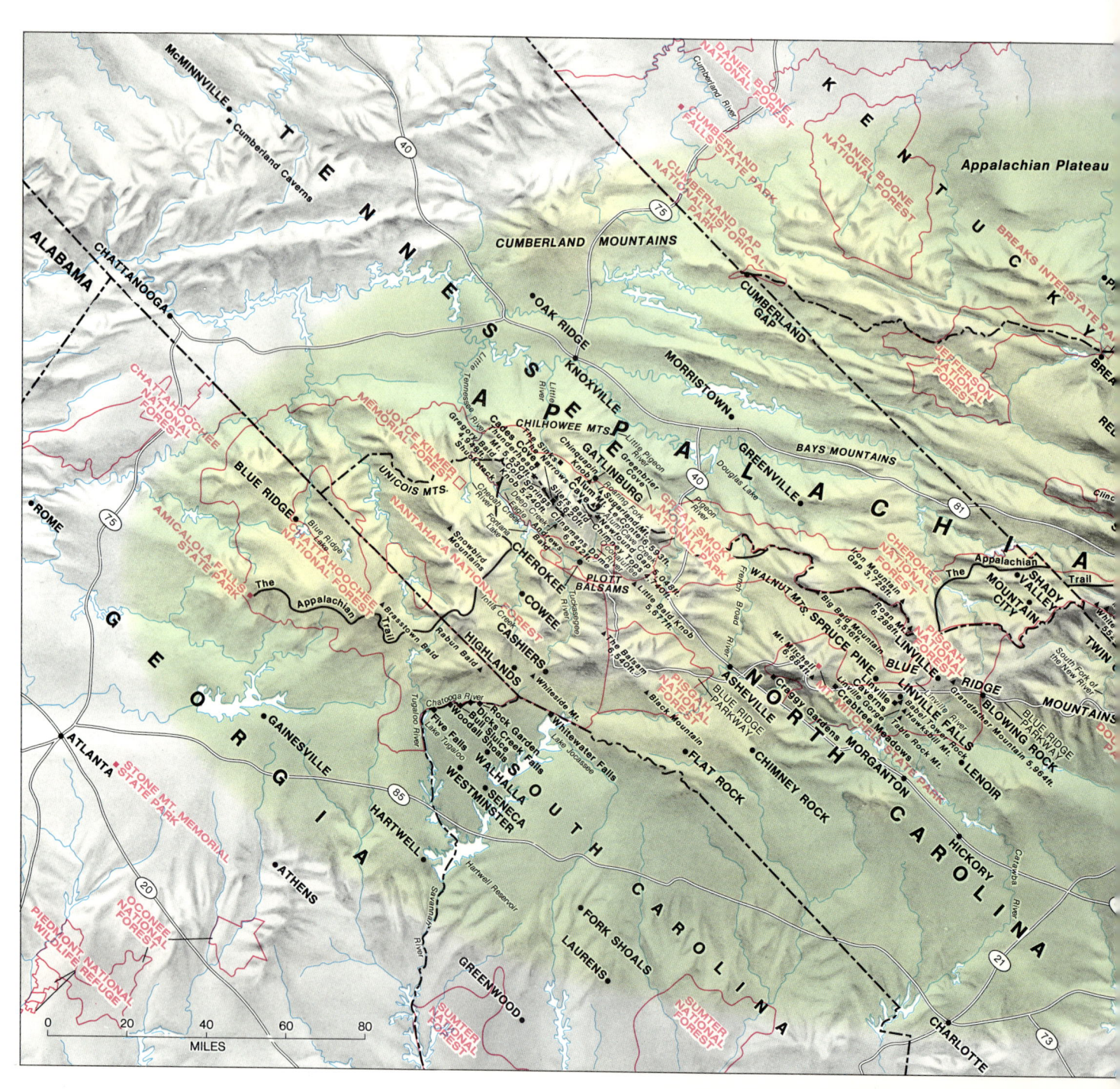

he gently rolling, wooded Southern Appalachians (shaded in the map at right) are capped with the most richly varied deciduous forest in North America. And fertile groves, broad valleys and myriad streams offer congenial habitats to a remarkable diversity of plant and animal life. On the detailed map below, elevations below 2,000 feet appear in dark green, between 2,000 and 4,000 feet in yellow green, and over 4,000 feet in white. The region's national parks and forests are outlined in red, rivers and streams are shown as blue lines, and mountain peaks by black triangles. The black squares denote points of special interest, including waterfalls and some of the area's many caves. Black dots designate towns. A segment of the Appalachian Trail, which runs from Maine to Georgia, is marked by a solid black line; and the scenic Blue Ridge Parkway unobtrusively rides the crest of the chain for 469 miles from Virginia to North Carolina.

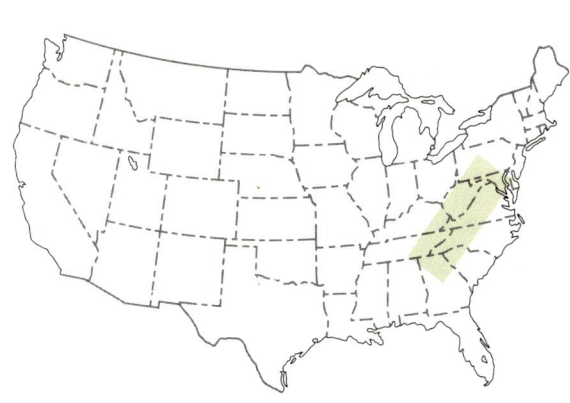

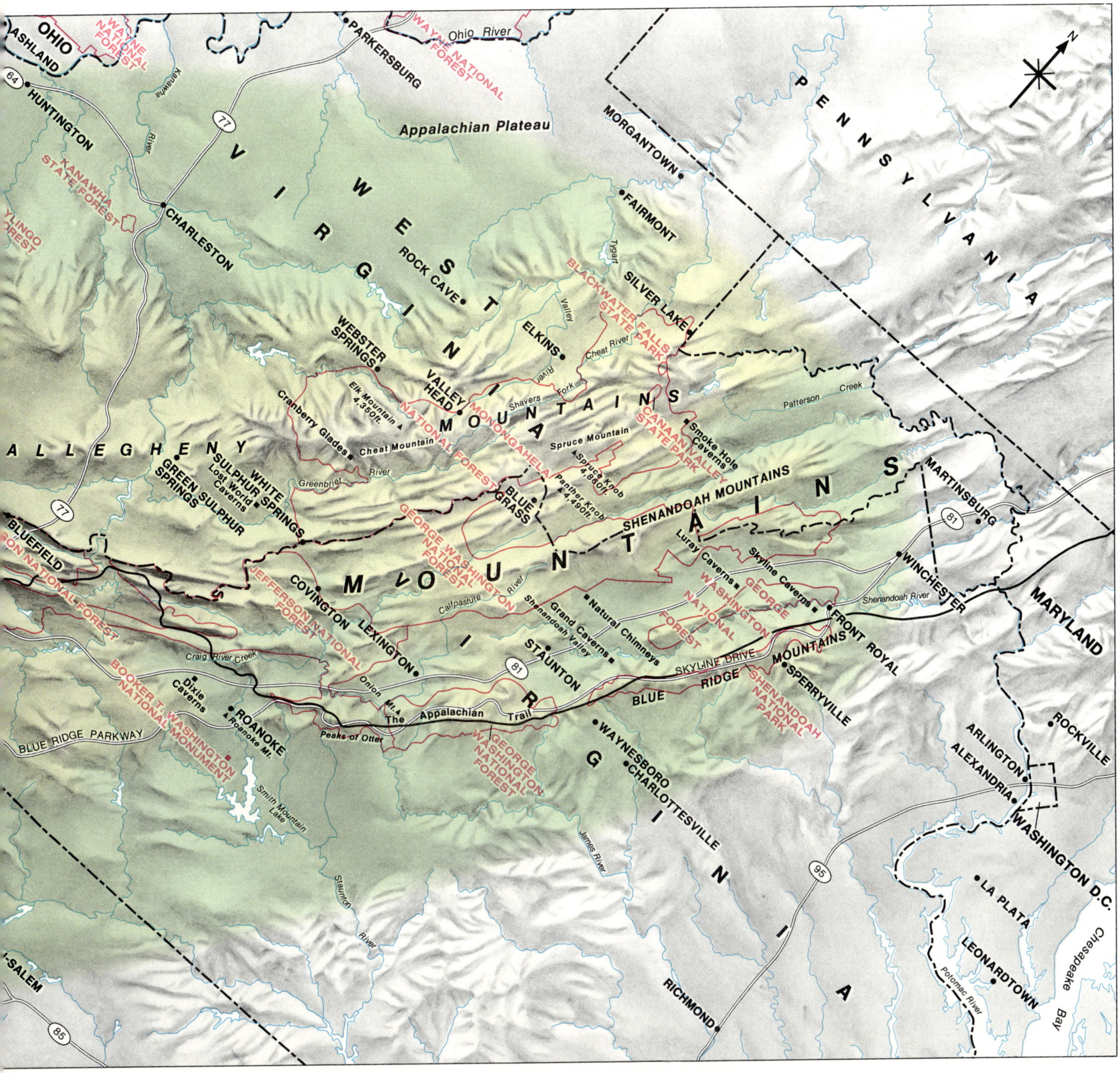

1/ Mountains of Subtle Majesty

For the mountain being cloven asunder, she presents to your eye, through the cleft, a small catch of smooth blue horizon... inviting you... to pass through the breach and participate of the calm below. THOMAS JEFFERSON/ NOTES ON VIRGINIA

All day long, pictures of things pass through my eyes and disappear, somewhere inside. Pictures of stop signs, falling leaves, Form 1040s, green fields, superhighways, the blue of heaven, the gray of garbage cans, everything, all unreel forever. Only once in a while will a frame lodge in my mind for good, and I never know why that particular frame. But there it is. I still have one that stopped and stayed on a day in 1960.

It was a day in deep summer, not long after breakfast time when the heat begins to weigh down on northern Virginia. I had been walking up an old fire road toward the top of a hill in Rappahannock County. I no longer remember why I was walking along the dirt road; probably I was just fooling around in the woods with nothing special in mind.

Near the top of the hill I came upon the picture that caught in my mind and remains today. It was nothing really, nothing more than an opening in the woods to the west, with the ground dropping away very steeply. No rain had fallen for weeks, and the leaves underfoot were crisp. Where I stood I was above the level of the treetops farther down the slope. In one of the trees a flick of red and black and white caught my eye: a pileated woodpecker. Out in front unfolded a pastoral scene: farms, wood lots, rolling fields, all still and slumberous under the sun's heat. In the distance, miles away, rose a long and hazy line of mountains —the crest of the Southern Appalachians.

A little thing, I told you. Little mountains, too, really. The piece of the Appalachian system I saw that day was the northern portion of a long, meandering range called the Blue Ridge, in whose foothills I lived in those days, not too far from the town of Sperryville. There the mountains climb to not much more than 4,000 feet. Farther south in Tennessee and North Carolina, some of the crests are higher, though still not tall as mountains go. The highest point in the Southern Appalachians—as well as the tallest peak east of the Mississippi River—is North Carolina's Mount Mitchell, in a subdivision of the Blue Ridge called the Black Mountains. Yet Mitchell is only 6,684 feet at its crown.

Modest mountains, then, the Southern Appalachians. But that picture of the Blue Ridge stays with me anyway, while pictures of the Alps and the Rockies have flickered on through my mind and are gone. Why that should be, I don't know. Maybe it is because I was raised in the Appalachians and am therefore made uneasy by the theatrical quality of more imposing ranges. Look at us, the Alps and the Rockies seem to say. See how jagged and savage and grand we are. But my mountains, the Southern Appalachians, are not so flashy. Their understated beauty asks for a finer eye. Their scale is not awe inspiring, but human; their charm not striking, but subtle. Yet these mountains possess a classic elegance, a regularity of form, a graceful symmetry in the rounded, rolling heights, covered in green to their summits.

The entire chain of the Appalachians—named by Hernando de Soto after a tribe of Florida Gulf Coast Indians, the Apalachee—stretches from central Alabama all the way north to Newfoundland, roughly paralleling the eastern shoreline of the continent for 2,000 miles. At a quick glance, the system seems much the same from one end to the other. But ever since my days as a teenager in northern Virginia, it is the southerly end of the range that has held a particular appeal for me. My geologist friends tell me, and no doubt they are scientifically correct, that the true border of the Southern Appalachians is the defile sliced through the mountains by the Roanoke River in southern Virginia. But I think of the dividing line as the Pennsylvania border.

In their east-to-west profile, the Southern Appalachians comprise a complex but well-charted system that starts at a boundary called the Fall Line. This is a line connecting the points where waterfalls and rapids made further boat travel impractical for early settlers—and where they established their major population centers: Richmond, Petersburg, Raleigh, Columbia, Augusta and Macon. Rising slowly west of this line is a shallow staircase of low hills known as the Piedmont; I was in the Piedmont on that summer day in Rappahannock County, Virginia. Looking into the western distance at the Blue Ridge, I was seeing the spine of the Southern Appalachians, which stretched far out of my vision, north to Pennsylvania and south into Georgia. Farther west beyond the Blue Ridge lies a broad belt of lower folds called the Valley and Ridge Province; still farther west stands the last escarpment, the Alleghenies, which peter out to the west into a broad band of eroded hills.

To my eye, the most beautiful and dramatic part of the entire system, north or south, east or west, is the high, richly forested Blue Ridge. And if I had to be more specific, I would narrow my preference down to that intriguing museum of natural history that makes up its best-known subdivision, the Great Smoky Mountains—all sweeping troughs and billows of soft, inviting foothills and remote, mysterious peaks.

Perhaps more than any other factor, the passing of the seasons emphasizes for me the glories of these mountains. When wild flowers begin to bloom in early spring the higher summits emerge from the snow, frost and fog of winter to become as colorful as a crazy quilt. The blanket of blossoms—flame azalea, yellow fringed orchid, orange trumpet creeper, blue-purple monkshood—grows more profuse as summer approaches and species after species bursts into flower. By September the trees in the mountains' great deciduous canopy begin to dominate the display with colors that easily rival the wild flowers'.

Threading through this botanical wonderland is a lacework of streams and small rivers in such numbers that many remain nameless. Waterfalls tumble over ledges. Among the rolling mountains are anomalous and intriguing patches of land and flora with special names: gently sloping or flat areas called coves at the bottoms of mountain valleys and hundreds of so-called heath balds, high-altitude open patches where hardy flowering shrubs form carpets of color every spring.

Although European immigrants have settled and farmed and logged in and around the Southern Appalachians for well over 150 years, enormous tracts remain much as they were when only the Indians hunted or planted small corn patches here. Partly the preservation stems from the rough and densely overgrown terrain, which is not compatible with large-scale cultivation and commerce. Partly it is the result of a long-established and jealously guarded system of national and state parks, begun in 1915 with Mount Mitchell State Park, and today embracing protected enclaves totaling millions of acres. These parks and the wild land around them make up perhaps the most accessible of our great wilderness areas. Not only are the fringes easy to get to from the huge pop-

Mountains of Subtle Majesty /23

A white-tailed deer—the only species of deer in the Southern Appalachians—nibbles young oak leaves at West Virginia's Cheat River.

ulation centers of the East Coast and the Midwest, but the visitor finds that even their deepest reaches can be penetrated easily in a day's hike from a road. The 514,668-acre Great Smoky Mountains National Park begins at the city limits of Gatlinburg, Tennessee.

Four of the tallest peaks in the Southern Appalachians—Grandfather Mountain, Clingmans Dome, Roan Mountain and Mount Mitchell—can be reached, or nearly so, by automobile. And for 469 miles, a meandering highroad called the Blue Ridge Parkway rides the crest of the Southern Appalachians from near Waynesboro, Virginia, into North Carolina all the way to the doorstep of the Great Smokies, which themselves are traversed by a road.

These roads scarcely belong in a wild place, but they do represent a reasonable way to open the mountains' natural beauties to less adventurous visitors. The visitors rarely venture far off the road; a few hundred yards to each side the wilderness resumes. And the Blue Ridge Parkway is incomparably more beautiful than most highways: only two lanes wide, the forest coming nearly to its edge. Along its route the parkway offers access to hundreds of turnouts, scenic overlooks and trails.

Early one September morning I entered the parkway near Roanoke. My ultimate destination—after a short detour—was Great Smoky Mountains National Park 359 miles away. There was a light fog, turning the world soft gray. I drove a while in the quiet morning, and as the fog began to burn away, I spotted a baby box turtle lumbering like a two-inch tank across the deserted road. I pulled the car over and stopped to take a look. When I reached for the turtle it pulled in its head and then locked up altogether by closing the hinged forward part of its bottom shell. The action made a soft hiss, like that of some door-closing devices. The hiss is caused by substantially the same thing: closing the hinged gate reduces the space inside the shell and squeezes a small sigh of air out of the turtle's lungs.

I carried the turtle over to a rocky ledge to take its picture. By then the animal had reopened the built-in drawbridge of its orange and black castle and was scrabbling around, getting out of position every time I focused on it. In the process of trying to zero in on it I had to pay such close attention to the ledge area around it that I spotted something I would otherwise have missed. It was one of those curious insects called walkingsticks, four inches long and yet so perfectly camouflaged as a dead twig as to be nearly undetectable. Walkingsticks, members of the same order as crickets, grasshoppers, mantises and cockroaches, are hatched in spring, colored green to match the foliage. But by fall they have passed through several molts and taken on the autumnal grayish tan of the insect before me. Once my eyes had become used to the shape of the one walkingstick, I was able to see four or five more on the same ledge—a little colony that had at first looked like a random jumble of dried twigs. In case their camouflage fails, walkingsticks have a second line of defense: they squirt out a substance that acts as a repellent to some predator insects.

I left the turtle and the walkingsticks behind and went back along my way—to stop again, quickly, when I saw a black line scribbling itself across the road. I have never been able to resist a reptile of any kind, much less a snake. So I jumped out and caught up with this one—a black rat snake—before it could get off the shoulder of mowed grass and into the woods. I treated the snake with respect even though it was nonvenomous, because an old veteran of the same species had once come right at me across a Virginia clearing; it was a scarred six footer with part of its tail missing, and it made great, scything strikes in the air as it advanced. I had never seen a snake coming for a man, even when the man had provoked the snake, as I had that one. Now I provoked this smaller one, too, by blocking its way to the woods. It proved to be tough but not really aggressive. It hissed, and vibrated its tail to make a buzzing sound, then struck when I came too close. But then I backed off, and it slid away into the woods.

By midmorning, the fog had risen and I drove under broken cloud cover. Now and then the sun would break through, stunning me with its unexpectedness and delighting me with its brilliance so that I stopped at whatever overlook was handy just then. Sometimes I would find myself gazing over a stretch devoid of any sign of man, a great sweep of mountains, with tendrils of fog snaking up from the far-off forests to disappear into the momentary blue. More often, past the forested slopes, there would be fields or farms visible in the distance.

Toward the end of the afternoon, I had reached the Plott Balsam Mountains of North Carolina, a short subdivision of the Smokies not much more than 10 miles long, named after a family of early settlers. The clouds had been mainly driven off by a chill wind. But it was getting late; the light was starting to fade and I stopped by a darkening grove of tall pines to take some last pictures. As I walked toward the grove I heard a *whuff* in among the pines, the sound that a fighter makes when he is hit unexpectedly in the stomach or, in this case, that a deer makes when it is startled into sudden flight. There were two of them, does. Their white rumps made it easy to follow their flight through the trees, only 20 or 30 yards down the hill, before they stopped in the dusk. I stalked the does the best I could, and they let me get close enough for a last good look before they crashed off down the steep, tangled pitch of the mountain.

Elsewhere, back in the forest, though rarely if ever seen by parkway travelers, are black bears and the European wild boar, the latter introduced to the mountains in 1912 and currently flourishing to the extent that farmers in some fringe areas regard it as a nuisance. Occasionally scattered reports come in of bobcats and even cougars, but these tough, skittish predators are seldom seen near civilization here, and only rarely in the wild. Smaller mammals are abundant—gray and red foxes, raccoons, skunks and opossums; so, too, are rodents of all kinds, most visibly the chipmunk. The bird population, both native and migratory, is enormous. An ornithologist once counted 22 species of warblers breeding on a single mountain in West Virginia. Hawks and grouse are very common; the endangered golden eagle still soars the heights. And the once-threatened wild turkey is coming back strongly under stiff laws controlling hunting and the use of pesticides.

In the waning light I saw no more wildlife along the parkway. By suppertime I arrived in the little town of Highlands, North Carolina, just inside the high southeastern rim of the Blue Ridge and close to the South Carolina-Georgia border. The altitude at Highlands is nearly 4,000 feet, with higher mountains all around. The prevailing warm winds come in from the Gulf Stream, heavy with water, and pass without much let or hindrance over Georgia and South Carolina. Then the taller mountains, which include the Highlands country, force the moist winds up into cold altitudes. Since the chilled air can hold less water vapor, rain is wrung from the winds. In some years Highlands gets almost 100 inches of precipitation, more than any place in the United States except the Pacific Northwest, and the proliferation of trees and plants in the area offers striking evidence of the effect of that much moisture.

The same general situation holds true, though to a lesser extent, throughout much of the Southern Appalachians. The highest parts of the mountains receive enormous amounts of rain, far more than many of the prevailing trees, shrubs and flowers would need simply to survive, and as a result the overall composition of the forest in most places is far more lush and complex than it would be with, say, half the rainfall. Clingmans Dome, for example, where red spruce and Fraser fir flourish, sometimes receives an annual precipitation of 85 inches although these dominant conifers require only 15 to 20 inches to survive. This lavish watering makes the Southern Appalachians a sort of enormous botanical garden; in the Smokies alone there are over 100 native species of trees; 15 to 20 of them reach record size there. And an extraordinary variety of forest communities exist cheek by jowl, rising from the sheltered valleys up to the wind-battered mountaintops.

In a single day a hiker in the Southern Appalachians can pass through a host of these communities, making the botanical, climatological and zoological equivalent of a trip from Georgia to Canada. I did so, starting one October day in Gatlinburg at an elevation of 1,400 feet, on a warm, still morning when the temperature was 68° F. Immediately to the south and east, the Great Smoky Mountains rose for almost a vertical mile. The average temperature on the way up these mountains drops by 2.25° per 1,000 feet of additional elevation. Thus the temperature on top of Mount Le Conte—the tallest peak and my destination this day—would be about the same as in the woods outside Winnipeg or Montreal, 1,000 miles farther north.

Called the Grandstand of the Smokies for the view from its summit, Mount Le Conte is only a few miles inside the park. Not long after leaving Gatlinburg I found myself on an upward-leading forest path called the Alum Cave Bluffs Trail. In the slanting fall sunlight I paused for a moment to watch a half dozen comma butterflies, named for the tiny silver marks that stand out on the underside of their mottled hind wings, basking on the trunks of yellow birch trees. They slowly opened and closed their richly colored brown and mauve and yellow wings; from time to time they would flutter off into the air and then settle back again on the tree trunk they had just left.

The butterflies and I were on the edge of a small cove of approximately 15 acres, one of many in the eroded limestone of these mountains. Both sides of this cove, typically, were protected by ridges forming a sort of wide funnel down which rain or meltwater had long been channeled. The water had brought billions of soil particles down from the mountain to this piece of flatter terrain. There the particles had settled into an alluvial fan of deep soil, although the outlines of this fan—and of most others in the Southern Appalachians—were obscured by vegetation that flourished in the fertile earth.

Because of the richness of the soil, coves were often the first pockets of ground to be cleared and planted by early settlers; but the one through which I was walking seemed never to have been cut over. All

28/ Mountains of Subtle Majesty

Buckled in a classic example of mountain-folding, the Great Smokies, highest portion of the Blue Ridge, are lightly dusted with snow.

around me were tree species that local naturalists refer to collectively as cove hardwoods. The tallest were the yellow birches that towered to a height of 80 feet and more. The smallest trees were birches, too, saplings whose leaves had taken on a frizzy look from a few light nighttime frosts, as if a flame had passed rapidly over them. The leaves were still green, but their toothed edges had turned up, making each into a tiny, wide-bottomed boat. In between the saplings and the mature birches was a dense mosaic of basswoods, yellow buckeyes and sugar maples. Spires of sunlight knifed down between their branches, briefly illuminating the shade of the forest floor. Down there, in a tangle of lesser plants, everything seemed to be clambering on everything else, scrabbling and scratching to get near the sun.

The most successful of the scramblers was the rosebay rhododendron, a tough shrub whose twisted, ropy trunk can grow as thick as a man's upper arm, its leathery leaves glistening dark green as if they had been oiled. The rhododendron grows rankly in these mountains. It even germinates in the leaf mold caught in cracks or crotches high in the trees, sending roots down the flanks of its host. On the ground it forms thickets within the woodland so tangled and difficult of passage that local people refer to them, unfondly, as hells. As the trail climbed across the cove, it took me through a series of these rhododendron hells. In them the shade—both from the thickets' leaves and those of the canopy overhead—was so deep that hardly anything but seedlings of the rhododendrons themselves had been able to take root.

The trail ran along Alum Cave Creek, a pleasant little watercourse that emerges from beneath some bluffs higher up and joins the West Prong of the Little Pigeon River, which eventually flows out of the park near Gatlinburg. On September 1, 1951, the runoff from a cloudburst on the mountain carried hundreds of whole trees from the heights above, leaving scars from landslides on the flanks of Mount Le Conte. During the fury of the storm Alum Cave Creek itself became a torrent that swept away other trees, carrying them far down the mountain.

At the moment, however, Alum Cave Creek was chuckling prettily and inoffensively over the rocks, and seemed incapable of having participated in such havoc. But evidence of the flood was all around me. Tree trunks, many years old but so thick they had not yet completely rotted, lay stacked at odd angles on the ground—logs in a jam whose river had run dry. Mixed among them was a jumble of older debris, from countless other floods over the ages, decomposing to make the cove even richer. The lines of the logs were softened by a thick green blanket of moss. Under this blanket the wood was decayed enough so that yellow-birch seedlings had been able to take root along the tops of some of the logs, known as nurse logs because they provide nourishment for new trees. Eventually the nurse logs would rot away entirely, leaving the birch trees standing on stilt roots.

I made my way on up the trail through fire cherry and spruce until I came to a rocky knob, free of trees but covered by rhododendron, azalea, mountain laurel and sand myrtle. All these hardy shrubs belong to a family of plants called heaths; throughout the Southern Appalachians there are patches of land like this one that have acquired the name heath balds, devoid of trees but covered by a thick profusion of shrubs. No one is certain, but a few scientists think heath balds (also known as laurel slicks to some local residents) establish themselves in areas first denuded by lightning-caused fires. A more generally accepted conclusion is that heath balds appear on exposed slopes and ridges where precipitation is quickly lost through surface runoff, leaving the area particularly vulnerable to the desiccating effects of the wind—not an ideal situation for trees, but one the sturdy heaths can cope with easily. Moreover, they thrive on such scanty, acidic soils as that on the shale knob on which I stood. During winter the azaleas drop their foliage, but all the other heaths keep their leaves year round, sometimes furled inward in below-freezing weather to reduce exposed area to a minimum. Then, in spring, the larger heath balds blaze out in displays of pink, red, purple and white blossoms that have become famous among horticulturists—pink beds of mountain laurel and azalea near Asheville, expanses of purple rhododendron on Roan Mountain.

The little bald I had encountered soon gave way to the forest again. Around a bend I came on Alum Cave Bluffs, a large shale overhang that is near the source of the stream. The place is named for the alum salts —formed by the oxidation of natural pyrites into sulfuric acid and then into alum salts—that effloresce on the surface of the outcropping. The alum occurs in very small quantities, but when I walked over to the outcropping I could see the white, powdery mineral crusted there. There is a persistent legend that the Confederate Army attempted to dig alum out of the rocks here to make gunpowder during the Civil War, but it is generally agreed that the story is false, possibly inspired by the existence of nearby caves whose walls are caked with saltpeter.

Not far past the bluffs, I entered the shade of a spruce and fir forest that continued to the summit of Mount Le Conte. On top, I came to the

32/ Mountains of Subtle Majesty

Beyond a hoarfrost-laden tree, the first pallid light of a February dawn illuminates snow-covered mountains on the Tennessee-North

Carolina border. In the distance, Mount Mitchell, whose summit dominates the Black Mountains, stands majestically above the clouds.

rough lodge and bunkhouses that are maintained there by a concessionnaire under contract to the National Park Service. Food is carried up by pack train, as are some of the guests. Others hike. The lodge is usually booked up far in advance, and I had not been able to reserve a bunk. But there was enough food so that I could have supper. Afterward I found my way a few hundred yards down a dark trail to the National Park Service shelter, a roofed, three-sided rectangle of stone, where a number of other backpackers had already unrolled their sleeping bags. The shelter is all that will remain in a few years, as the National Park Service plans to tear down the lodge and its outbuildings to restore the wilderness character of the area.

Next morning I got up early and went to a lightly frosted clearing in the forest to watch the sunrise. The Great Smokies lay all in front of me, the bulks of them hidden in the clouds. The tops reared through this soft, misty sea, at first pink and pearly, and then changing slowly to the color of pale flame. Then the sky turned blue, and the sea became just white clouds again. But still they hid most of the mountainsides, leaving only the tops in the sun's warmth like scattered outposts in the sky.

All around me was a faint but pervasive odor that some people compare to that of a skunk but that I find not at all unpleasant. It came from a wild flower called Rugel's ragwort. It is also called Smoky Mountains ragwort, because it is found nowhere else, although conditions for its growth would seem to be almost identical at similar altitudes in a hundred other places.

A species like this ragwort that exists only in a certain locality is called an endemic. The Southern Appalachian region is full of them, both plants and animals, for a number of fascinating prehistorical reasons that have also caused northern and southern species to mingle here in profusion. During the various ice ages, the last ending only some 10,000 years ago, northern plants and animals that had been forced out of their normal habitat by the cold of the glaciers found new homes in these mountains and valleys. Although now the nearest true timberline is hundreds of miles to the north, the Southern Appalachians were much colder then; there were almost surely treelines on many of these mountains. Below the treeline, on the lower slopes and in the valleys of the southern mountains, the climate was cool enough for the displaced northern species to thrive.

But then the glaciers withdrew, and the warm air took over at lower altitudes. In the new climate, northern plants and animals could sur-

The four salamanders at right, common in the Southern Appalachians, represent two of the seven families of their amphibian class. Each family has its distinguishing characteristics: the red-cheeked and Blue Ridge Mountain salamanders, of the lungless family, respire through the skin and mouth lining. The spotted and marbled mole salamanders spend almost all of their lives underground.

Mountains of Subtle Majesty /35

RED-CHEEKED SALAMANDER

SPOTTED SALAMANDER

BLUE RIDGE MOUNTAIN SALAMANDER

MARBLED SALAMANDER

vive only in the cool habitats of the uplands, and thus wound up more or less marooned atop the higher mountain masses. For example, the forest of Fraser fir surrounding my clearing on top of Mount Le Conte is almost identical to the stands of balsam fir that dominate so much of the Maine woods. Thus, species that had existed as homogeneous populations covering wide areas became dozens of smaller populations, broken up and cut off from each other by the warmer lowland climate between peaks or mountain masses.

The more mobile species that could take to the air literally had a way out of the situation. Plants and fungi with windborne seeds or spores, birds and flying insects, all these could escape isolation. But for more fragile or earthbound forms of life—herbs, wingless insects, snakes—each outpost in the mountains became a small Darwinian laboratory where species evolution was almost forced to go its own separate path. The result has been the gradual development of an extraordinary number of species: 200 different trees, shrubs, mosses and lichens and 40 wild-flower species flourish in the Southern Appalachians.

However the classic example of species evolving in isolation is not among the plants but rather among a branch of the amphibian class: salamanders, humble creatures that nonetheless possess what might seem an inexplicably strong appeal for naturalists. "I don't know how to impart it," writes Maurice Brooks in his book *The Appalachians,* "but there is a strange fascination, a growing excitement in putting on old clothes, taking a collecting bag and a flashlight, and going mucking through a stream or wet woods on a rainy night to look for salamanders."

There are a dozen or more salamander species in the Southern Appalachians. Their habitats may be separated by only a few miles—but in those few miles are lowlands where conditions are not right for the salamanders' survival. And thus they have gone their separate evolutionary ways. Some are largely aquatic, others largely terrestrial. Some, including the pygmy salamander, climb tree trunks at night; others remain on the ground throughout their lives. Often the very species names make the point of their geographical isolation: the Yonahlossee salamander, for instance, named for a road on Grandfather Mountain, is found only east and north of the French Broad River in southwestern Virginia and North Carolina. And, for real isolation, the Peaks of Otter salamander is limited to two small mountains called Peaks of Otter, in Virginia's Blue Ridge—a mere dot on a distribution map.

Because of their secretive habits and drab coloration, salamanders are likely to go unnoticed by all but the most careful searcher. It is probable, then, that the vastness of the Southern Appalachians still harbors subspecies new to science. And more subspecies may be evolving even today. The red-cheeked salamander, for example, is a fairly ubiquitous type found at altitudes above 2,500 feet; but isolated populations of the same species, generally lacking the distinctive red cheek patches, crop up throughout the Southern Appalachians.

The morning was almost over, and it was time to start down Mount Le Conte. I went back to the shelter for my pack. When I set off the sun was already warm, but for a good way the trail still led through the cool shade of spruce and fir. I was watching my footing carefully in a steep part when I spotted a root that looked just enough different from the others to make me stop. It was a harmless ring-necked snake, a slate-colored squiggle about 18 inches long. These small, inoffensive reptiles are the most common snake of the Smokies and are abundant throughout the rest of the Southern Appalachians. At first I thought the animal was dead; even after I picked it up, it continued to feign death so well that I began to look for a wound. But when I put the snake down again it came to life, and wriggled down the steep pitch so frantically as to touch only here and there, like a stone skipping on water.

My diversion gone, I turned my attention back to the forest as I continued down the trail. Small mountain ash and fire cherry trees, both basically northern species and hence tough enough to live at high altitudes, were mixed in among the evergreens. An early frost had killed the ash and cherry leaves before they could change color. Many still hung on the branches, but others had fallen to the ground. The leaves on the trail, still a pale green like freeze-dried parsley, were so brittle they crunched to powder under my feet.

At one point, a ridge rose up to my right and I climbed up it. Through the trees I was able to get a view to the east. The mountains went off, rank after rank, until they disappeared in the smokelike haze that seems to breathe out of the forest. I was reminded of something I'd heard long ago, the remark of a mountain man who must have been standing in a forest much like this one. He had said he'd rather be a knot on a log up there than the mayor of the city down yonder. I could see why.

A Lush Botanical Mosaic

PHOTOGRAPHS BY SONIA BULLATY AND ANGELO LOMEO

From the earliest times, travelers in the Southern Appalachians recognized that these green forests sheltered an extraordinary treasury of flowering plants. Generations of botanists have since identified 2,500 trees, shrubs, mosses and lichens. Of these, 1,500 are flowering species—the greatest variety to be found in any comparably sized area in temperate North America.

One of the reasons for this diversity is the number of plant habitats in the Southern Appalachians, where elevations range from 900 feet above sea level to well over 6,000 feet. Shaped by runoff waters from rainfall that totals between 40 and 100 inches a year, the slopes of the mountains face in every direction —exposing the forests to varying hours of sunlight, holding and losing moisture as a result of evaporation at differing rates and maintaining a great range of temperatures. The rocky underpinnings of the mountains comprise granular dolomite, crumbly sandstone and hard graywacke; and the soils fluctuate across the pH scale from acid to neutral and in consistency from sandy to loamy.

The product of this complex interaction of conditions is flora that one botanist categorizes into 15 different vegetation communities. Two are unique to the region—they are called heaths and coves.

Heaths, which comprise massed displays of rhododendrons, laurels, myrtles and azaleas (pages 52-53), occur on the high slopes and in the understory of forests throughout the region. Colors range from a pinkish white to an intense purple, and the shiny, slick leaves provide a green carpet on the mountains throughout the entire year.

Coves are identified by their dominant form of vegetation: trees, among them, basswoods, oaks, maples and flowering redbuds (right). The deep, fertile soil of the coves, well watered by streams, also provides an ideal environment for flowering plants. Trumpet honeysuckle, crested dwarf iris, purple fringed orchid, dog hobble and columbine are a few among dozens. Cove wild flowers tend to be early bloomers—beginning in late February, the start of the Appalachian growing season, and lasting only until late May, when the leafy canopy of the trees closes overhead. But the display does not end, it only changes: from then until October other flora of the Southern Appalachians continues to provide the same color and enchantment.

REDBUD

40/ A Lush Botanical Mosaic

GOLDEN RAGWORT AND INDIAN PAINTBRUSH

A Refuge for Natives and Immigrants

The Southern Appalachians have traditionally formed a sort of hometown from which native wild flowers have traveled abroad, sometimes settling in distant lands. This emigration has been going on for some 350 million years, since these mountains rose to altitudes above the level of flooding and glaciation that were to cover much of the continent.

Among the many flowers whose progeny have wandered from home territory are fairy wand, columbine, Solomon's-seal and buttercup. These successful travelers can now be found growing in areas as far north as New England, westward to Illinois and south to Florida.

The Southern Appalachians nourish immigrants as well as emigrants. Because of the mountains' diverse habitats, wild flowers whose normal homes are far away also thrive here. Wood sorrel, for instance, is common to Canada, but also finds an unaccustomed Southern habitat in the Smokies; spiderwort, a familiar Western flower, maintains an outpost in the Southern Appalachians.

Finally, because of its protected isolation as much as its benign growing conditions, the area serves as a refuge for some endangered species: the delicate pink lady's-slipper has been picked so often by flower lovers in other parts of the country that it is being threatened with extinction; but it flourishes protected and largely undisturbed in the Southern Appalachian forests.

TRUMPET HONEYSUCKLE

FAIRY WAND

CRESTED DWARF IRIS

PINK LADY'S-SLIPPER

42/

COREOPSIS

BUTTERFLY WEED

SPIDERWORT

COLUMBINE

A Lush Botanical Mosaic /43

WOOD SORREL

BUTTERCUP

PURPLE FRINGED ORCHID

CANADA VIOLET

44/

BLEEDING HEART

SOLOMON'S-SEAL

A Lush Botanical Mosaic /45

FIRE PINK IN THE GRASS

DOG HOBBLE

WHITE-FRINGED PHACELIA

Endemics with Asian Cousins

About 200 species of plants native to the Southern Appalachians, including about 40 wild flowers, are found nowhere else in the world. These are endemics, plants that presumably evolved here and never traveled. The flowers on these pages are beautiful examples.

Endemic plants occur in every wilderness area: given enough time, some microenvironment is bound to breed a unique subspecies. But the Southern Appalachians appear to spawn a greater number than usual by virtue of the great age of the flora and the diversity of habitats folded within its hills.

An astonishing distinction of the Southern Appalachian flora is the fact that some of its endemic plants have close relatives in Asia (pages 48-49). The best explanation for this phenomenon, propounded by Aaron J. Sharp of the University of Tennessee, is that about 65 million years ago, when North America and Asia were connected by a land bridge across the Bering Strait, there was a great arclike range of similar vegetation that stretched from Southeast Asia through Siberia and Japan into Alaska and thence south and east in a sweeping curve into the Southern Appalachians. After the continents separated, long periods of glaciation scoured the north, and a subsequent drying period created the Great Plains of the Midwest, leaving the two groups of flora isolated half a world apart.

A Lush Botanical Mosaic /47

TRAILING PHLOX

48/

UMBRELLA MAGNOLIA

UMBRELLA LEAF

SILVER BELL

MAY APPLE

A Lush Botanical Mosaic /49

WITCH HOBBLE

A Lush Botanical Mosaic

FLAME AZALEA

Floral Epaulets on the Mountain Shoulders

The heaths that cloak many of the exposed ridges and peaks above 4,000 feet in the Southern Appalachians are among its chief glories. The word heath, a corruption of the Scottish word heather, was probably imported by early settlers from the British highlands, although no true heather grows in North America. The North American heath family consists of rhododendron, azalea, mountain laurel and mountain myrtle, as well as blueberry, huckleberry, male berry and wintergreen.

These plants are all found on Southern Appalachian heath balds, so named because they are largely bare of trees. (They are also called slicks by the mountain people, because of the shiny, smooth appearance of their leaves.) The smooth appearance is deceptive, however. These heath shrubs are usually three or four feet high and have tough, twisted stems; they present a tangled, almost impenetrable maze.

No one knows for sure how these heath balds originated; but experts speculate that the heaths may have replaced once-wooded areas that had been destroyed by a natural disaster such as a landslide or fire. Well suited to the shallow, acidic soil and tough enough to survive the force of the elements, the heath plants closed in on exposed land and crowded out other vegetation. Having established dominance, they now stand as jewels in the crown of Appalachian flowering life.

MOUNTAIN LAUREL

Atop a ridge in Great Smoky Mountains National Park stands a bank of catawba rhododendron, the one rhododendron species now endemic to the Southern Appalachians. Other rhododendrons native to the region are found throughout the Northeast, and their elegant, shiny leaves brighten woodlands north and south all year.

A Lush Botanical Mosaic /53

2/ An Ancient Mantle

I now entered upon the verge of the dark forest, charming solitude... inactivity and silence seem to pervade the earth. WILLIAM BARTRAM/ TRAVELS

The young botanist from Philadelphia had traveled nearly 300 miles by foot and horseback from the South Carolina coast to the mountains of western North Carolina to find new plants for the gardens of his wealthy Quaker brethren in England. Now he was warned that the Cherokee were skirmishing with frontiersmen on the western slopes of the Nantahala Mountains. To avoid the fighting, traders had recently left the area. William Bartram's attitude toward the Indians was trusting, however, and so he set out on a warm day in late May, 1775, to botanize the splendid forest all around him in the Southern Appalachians. A friend started with him early in the morning and they traveled together for nearly 15 miles through a stately forest of walnut trees and towering oaks mixed with maples and hickories. While they walked, Bartram carefully tallied and identified all the species in his notebook. In the afternoon, his friend turned back toward the nearest settlement, the town of Cowee on the Little Tennessee River. As Bartram continued westward, his solitude began to oppress him. He later wrote that he thought of himself as Nebuchadnezzar "expelled from the society of men, and constrained to roam in the mountains and wilderness."

Overheated and tired, Bartram finally halted on the bank of a small mountain stream, probably Iotla Creek. He was making a meal of a biscuit, some cheese and a bit of dried beef tongue when a strapping Indian youth, armed with a rifle and accompanied by two dogs, suddenly appeared from around a rocky shoulder of land. The Indian, clearly just as startled to find Bartram lolling on the grass as Bartram was to see him, stopped short. But then he smiled, strode toward Bartram and vigorously shook his hand. Bartram asked the way to the "Overhill towns" of the tribe, using the few words of Cherokee he had picked up. The Indian cheerfully pointed out the trail, they smoked some tobacco together and then again shook hands and parted. "He descended the hills, singing as he went," Bartram reported. Buoyed up by the encounter, the botanist continued his own journey.

The plant life that Bartram had been recording grew around him in astonishing profusion. He noted that deciduous trees he had studied farther north and along the coastal plain achieved spectacular proportions here in the Southern Appalachians. He walked through aisles of black oaks with furrowed trunks that he estimated at 30 feet in circumference at eye level. In places, massive chestnut trees as much as 13 feet thick at the base made up nearly 30 per cent of the forest. Columnar beeches and sweet gums swept up 150 feet, where their leaves joined the foliage of chestnuts and towering tulip trees to cut out all but the narrowest shafts of sun. Down on the forest floor, every day Bartram came upon new species—Indian olive bushes with fruit that was said to lure deer, Indian lettuce with pale yellowish-green leaves, fragrant *Magnolia auriculata*.

For a man with Bartram's unsuppressible curiosity about the wilderness and its plants, his month-long trek through the Southern Appalachians became a triumphant odyssey of discovery in what he came to call a "sublime forest." And today, two centuries after Bartram, a man can roam these woods with the same sense of wonder. By and large, enough is left so that the essential character of the forest remains despite the marks of settlers, the incursions of roads and loggers and even of calamitous plant diseases that have wiped out so many of the great trees of Bartram's day. Furthermore, today's botanizer views the Southern Appalachians from a vantage point of added knowledge that lends an extra measure of both excitement and satisfaction to his observation of the plants. For the fact was unknown to 18th Century scientists that the woodlands of the Southern Appalachians are an evolutionary remnant of the vast forest of flowering trees that covered much of the earth's land surface millions of years ago.

The forests of North America, Europe and Asia were once closely linked—like the continents themselves—in a great, broad-leafed community of trees during eons when the prevailing climate was one of lux-

56/ **An Ancient Mantle**

This elegant watercolor of a relative of the camellia was made by William Bartram who, with his father, John, discovered the tree in 1765 in Georgia. The naturalists named it Franklinia alatamaha, after the first citizen of their hometown, Philadelphia, and the river where they found the specimen. Apparently rare even when the Bartrams discovered it, the tree has become a cultivated variety but has not been seen in the wild since 1790.

uriant warmth. As the continental land masses began to drift apart, the forests became separated. Much later, when the climate cooled, advancing sheets of ice wiped out uncountable millions of trees in their path. New generations survived only by spreading farther and farther south. There was a curious pattern to this retreat that resulted, after tens of thousands of years, in a relative poverty of deciduous species in the forests of Europe, compared to those of Eastern North America.

The trees of Europe were caught in a trap. As they moved south in front of the ice they met the barrier of the Pyrenees, Alps and Caucasus, stretching from east to west directly across the path of survival. And any of the species that tried to climb the mountains ran into the cold of higher altitudes—which meant the death of many deciduous species that were not hardy enough to endure the change. By the end of the ice age some 10,000 years ago, there were only scattered pieces of the primeval European deciduous forest left. Some trees did manage to find a way through the mountains to survive on the southern slopes; to the west, others endured on sections of the continental shelf that were exposed as the earth's water became locked into ice sheets. And a few held out to the east in the ice-free slopes of the Balkans.

In North America, however, the warmth-loving deciduous trees had an escape route to the south. Here the mountains ranged in a generally north-south direction so that generations of trees were able to move before the ice and find refuge from the cold on the coastal plain and on the unglaciated southern slopes of the Appalachians. Some of the gigantic tulip trees and sweet gums that Bartram saw still stand in protected coves—the direct descendants of deciduous trees that have flowered season after season in these mountains for millions of years.

There is considerable dispute about just where many trees managed to survive in the Southern Appalachians during those chilly centuries—and indeed some argument about where on these mountains the glaciers may have extended. In 1973, for instance, two geologists from Appalachian State University reported that they had found evidence of glaciation—rock that was polished and grooved as though an ice sheet had passed over it—on Grandfather Mountain in the Blue Ridge. Later that year another group of scientists, dubious of the evidence, discovered an old lumberman in the area who explained that the grooves were carved by a steam-powered cable system that he had used to haul logs down the mountainside during the 1930s; some rusted cables were even found in the woods.

58/ **An Ancient Mantle**

Chestnut trees, averaging 20 feet in circumference, dwarf lumberjacks in the Great Smokies in a turn-of-the-century photograph.

There is no doubt, however, that as the ice age waned deciduous trees, well adapted to warm, humid growing conditions, flourished abundantly throughout the mountains. Today, the Great Smoky Mountains area alone, comprising a mere 800 square miles, is home to just about as many tree species—85 or so—as are found in all of Western Europe, which is 1,620 times as big.

In fact the only deciduous forests in the world equal in diversity to those of the Southern Appalachians occur in Eastern Asia. There, too, the mountains are on north-south axes. In addition, the immense Asian land mass dissipated the glaciers' flow so that ice sheets never probed south far enough to destroy much of the forest. Fascinatingly enough, some close relatives of the most distinctive trees of the Southern mountains, such as the tough and flexible hickories, the sprawling walnuts and the large-leafed magnolias, also grow natively in China, Taiwan and Japan. The magnificent tulip tree that prospers in the Southern Appalachians is native in only one other place outside Eastern North America: the forests of China. And none of these trees is native to Europe, although all of them have been introduced there since a troupe of brother botanists followed in Bartram's wake to explore the American wilderness for specimens to send home.

A prime incentive for this flowering of international botanical commerce was a book that Bartram published in 1791, in which he recorded his adventures in the Southern Appalachians. Editions of Bartram's *Travels* appeared in London, Dublin, France, Germany and Holland in rapid succession. Wordsworth read it and began writing poems about forests that he had never seen—"magnolia, spread/High as a cloud, high over head!" and "flowers that with one scarlet gleam/Cover a hundred leagues, and seem/To set the hills on fire."

Subsequently gentleman-botanists, adventurer-botanists and physician-botanists traveled to the Southern mountains, eager to catalogue this vast botanical garden. Not only could new plants be named, to the greater scientific glory of the discoverer, but some might also be added to the list of herbal medicines that then were a doctor's stock in trade. The greatest spur, however, was provided by royal patrons and wealthy merchants who wanted exotic new plants to enrich the royal parks and formal gardens of Europe.

France's Louis XVI sent one André Michaux and his son, François, to find new plants for the gardens of Versailles. Tagging along with them on their first expedition into the Southern mountains was a Scot,

John Fraser, who was working on his own. Growing competition between the two explorers one day prompted Michaux to pretend that he had lost his horses on the trail; he then encouraged Fraser to go on alone —the better for Michaux to keep sole credit for finding new species. Ironically Fraser, moving ahead, came on the fragrant balsam now called the Fraser fir, still abundant on Southern Appalachian summits.

Perhaps the most engaging and surely most colorful of the botanists was the luckless eccentric Constantine Samuel Rafinesque-Schmaltz. Born in Constantinople to a French father and a German mother and reared in Marseilles, Rafinesque-Schmaltz left France as a teenager during the Revolution. After several years of wandering, during which time he became fascinated with botany, he settled in Sicily. In 1815 wanderlust caught him again and he sailed for America. Just off the coast his ship was wrecked, but he managed to get ashore safely, though virtually penniless. Undismayed, he spent the next seven years collecting botanical samples in and around the Southern Appalachians.

The great naturalist-artist John James Audubon, who once encountered Rafinesque-Schmaltz along the Ohio River, described his new acquaintance's response to the discovery of a new plant: "I thought [he] had gone mad. He plucked the plants one after another, danced, hugged me to his arms, and exultingly told me that he had got, 'not merely a new species, but a new genus.'" Often Rafinesque-Schmaltz was wrong in his classifications, but when he died in 1840, too poor to pay his rent, he left behind a formidable herbarium, a collection of some 50,000 dried and labeled plants that testified to the wonders of the New World's virgin wilderness.

Besides its natural fecundity, the Southern Appalachian forest remained a rich botanical trove because man arrived here much later than he did in Europe and Asia. The aboriginal Indian population was never large, and its impact on the plants and trees was not harmful. The Cherokee in the Great Smoky Mountains actually cultivated trees: they were so fond of the caffeine-laden tea they brewed from the leaves of a holly tree they called yaupon, that they are said to have transplanted a grove to the mountains from the coastal plain. Even the first white settlers in the mountains did little damage. They cut what they needed for fuel and timber near their homesteads, but there was no drastic harm so long as the timbering was done by one man with an ax and horses or oxen to draw out the felled timber.

By the first years of the 20th Century, however, the big timber oper-

High in the spruce-fir forests of North Carolina

Mount Mitchell, loggers—seemingly unaware of their effect on the forest's ecology—pause for a 1913 photograph while loading felled timber.

ators had moved into the Southern mountains. They built logging roads and railroads to previously inaccessible fastnesses. Millions of hardwoods were hauled away for flooring, furniture making and the like; in later years pines and hemlocks went to the pulp mills.

Compared to the ravages of lumbering operations in other parts of the country, however, this harvest was late and not entirely lethal. Great sections were saved, either in their virgin state or with scatterings of the once-dominant trees, while the marvelous complexity of the understory survived virtually intact. At the time the half-million-acre Great Smoky Mountains National Park came under the protection of the federal government in 1934, for example, 40 per cent of the area was still untouched by logging. (There has been no logging at all in the area since 1939.) Unfortunately, in the other 60 per cent, harsh traces of the timbering operations of the early 1900s will remain for centuries —especially in stretches where spruce and fir were stripped away.

Some of these scars are noticeable along the Appalachian Trail, a 2,000-mile footpath that links the mountain peaks from Maine to Georgia. They are particularly evident near Newfound Gap, right in the center of the park. On the Tennessee side to the northwest the evergreen forest is still intact; the spruce and fir begin about 1,000 feet below the ridge-top trail and continue in an unbroken mantle of green to the summit. But on the slopes that drop away to the southeast, toward North Carolina and the industrialized and populated Piedmont areas, these valuable softwood trees have been cut down. In their stead are young deciduous trees. So long as they are undisturbed, spruce and fir cling successfully to their existence on these high slopes of the Appalachians; they flourish and replenish themselves with new seedlings. But when the trees are cut or blown down or burn away naturally, swift-growing fire cherry usually sprouts in their place, with a mass of spindly branches that elbow out most competition. Within 25 years, the fire cherry grows up to 40 feet tall; then it usually dies off—to be replaced by yellow birch, mountain ash and other slower-growing but longer-lived deciduous trees.

One autumn day, early in the morning, I was hiking along a section of the trail called Mollies Ridge. The mountains stretched away below me till they disappeared in the mist. I felt very remote indeed on the 4,500-foot-high ridge. But loggers had been there too, deep in the Smokies, and well into this century to judge by the fact that the trunks of most of the trees were less than a foot thick. Here and there, jagged against the slim, vertical lines of the new growth, were ancient oaks and yellow birches. Thick branches grew out of them, often horizontal at first and then dipping groundward at crazy angles. The trees were knotty, gnarled things, splaying crooked joints and zigzag twigs in every direction. They looked as though they might reach out and snatch me one night in the dark of the moon with a crackle of brittle fingers. But to a lumberman those old trees would seem more pitiable than sinister; in fact, they were the malformed culls that the loggers of years ago scorned to fell.

Yet all through the Southern Appalachians there are stands of forest that look much as they did when Europeans first saw them. One such pocket is Greenbrier Cove, in eastern Tennessee. The cove itself is a scoop in the southwest slope of 4,800-foot Greenbrier Pinnacle, sheltered by an amphitheater of 6,000-foot peaks to the south. Hoping that a visit to the cove would give me some notion of what the first explorers saw, I made arrangements to spend a day hiking with Zenith Whaley, a farmer and outdoorsman who was born in the Greenbrier section before it became a protected wilderness area. He was eager to visit a giant old tree that he hadn't seen in a good many years; he called it a yellow poplar, just as all local folk call its kind. Actually *Liriodendron tulipifera* is not a poplar but a tulip tree, the tallest hardwood in North America. Some reach heights of 200 feet, adorning the springtime slopes of the Southern Appalachians with big sun-filled blossoms.

We approached the cove along an old dirt road that ran through second-growth woods: closely set magnolia, walnut and maple trees not more than a foot in diameter. The trees became bigger and bigger as we left the dirt road and worked our way up the lower reaches of Greenbrier Pinnacle. And I began to notice, too, a great number of dead trees, still standing. "See that snag over there?" Zenith said, pointing to a tree whose top had broken off. "And those other ones off there? All chestnut." They probably had been dead since about 1930, for that was when the greatest botanical disaster in recorded North American history—the chestnut blight—appeared this far south; by 1950 it had destroyed more than 90 per cent of the chestnuts in the forest.

I'm too young ever to have seen the chestnut trees before the blight, when they were at full strength in the Southern mountains. But what a sight it must have been. The great naturalist Donald Culross Peattie recollected a July day in the early 1900s gazing down "from the slopes of Mount Mitchell at the coves of the Craggies, upon the whole forest, far as eye could see, tossing with the creamy blooms of the chestnut. . . .

They were so many, the chestnuts, and each crown bore such a myriad of long shining catkins, that as the wind threshed those woods the whole sea of waving leaves seemed breaking into whitecaps."

Nowadays, living chestnut trees appear in the Southern Appalachians only as shoots growing from old stumps. The shoots start out vigorously enough, sometimes growing as high as 25 feet, and the long, elegant, toothed leaf is still common in the forest's understory. Although I have never seen it, I'm told that occasionally a tree will bear a meager crop of nuts. But before the trunk is even a foot wide, the blight strikes and the saplings die.

The blight is spread by a fungus that was accidentally introduced around the turn of the century into the New York City area on an imported Chinese chestnut tree, and gradually worked its way throughout the East. The fungus penetrates the tree wherever there is a small wound and then infects the bark, through whose inner layer the sap returns from the leaves down to the roots to sustain the living tree. As the diseased bark forms cankers that girdle the trunk, the flow of sap stops and the tree dies above the girdle—though its root system continues to send out new shoots, and its hard core remains unaffected, often holding the trunk upright for years. Though the disease has affected every single chestnut grove in America, nevertheless it is possible that my sons in their lifetime may yet see the sight that Peattie remembered. Researchers have recently discovered a strain of fungus that robs the blight-causing fungus of its virulence. There is some small hope that the new strain can be made to take hold in the wild.

"It'd be wonderful if they could do something," Zenith said. "Best tree we had. Take a look at this log here." With his jackknife he dug into what looked like a thoroughly rotted chestnut log lying on the forest floor. An inch under the surface the wood was perfectly sound. The heartwood of a chestnut tree, rich in a natural preservative called tannin, is almost impervious to fungi and weathering. In consequence, logs from long-dead trees such as this are still salvaged from the woods and used for flooring, fencing or interior paneling.

As we continued our climb, tulip trees appeared all around us, mixed with splashes of red maple, yellow buckeye and an occasional stately silver-bell tree—the latter named for the distinctive shape of the white flowers that swing from its branches in the spring. Somewhere among these tulip trees was the one Zenith was searching for, and I was beginning to feel that nothing less than miraculous luck would let him find it in this dense forest. But he seemed imperturbably confident.

"We'll just go on up there a little ways and have a look," he said. In a few minutes we found ourselves deep in a giant snarl of rhododendron, fallen logs, and the greenbrier that gives this part of the woods its name. Greenbrier is a long vine, whose tough green stems are covered with thorns; its small leaves are borne only at the end of the vine, at the tops of the shrubs around which the greenbrier twines. For perhaps a quarter of an hour we climbed and crawled and shoved our way through thickets, like ants clambering through tangled grass.

When we finally fought free we stopped to take a break. Near us was a "grayback"—one of the giant sandstone boulders that lie scattered through the Southern Appalachian forest. Sometimes they are found together in boulder fields, but often they just sit all alone, like this one. Pried loose from the upper slopes by frost action, they then crawl down the mountainsides for centuries, edged along inch by inch by gravity and the alternate freezing and thawing of the soil. Though graybacks as high as 25 feet have been found in these mountains, the one near us was only about six feet. I walked around to the back of it and on the other side discovered that windborne soil had lodged on top of the rock in sufficient quantity to provide footing for a matty growth of red-berried wintergreen, and for me. Once on top, I bent over and a little soundless explosion suddenly went off in my face. I had disturbed a nest under the ground-hugging leaves and mice began springing out like clowns from a circus car. I suppose there were no more than three or four but they seemed to be coming by the dozen as one after another they went bouncing over the edge of the high boulder like little brown Ping-Pong balls and disappeared among the leaves of the forest floor. Feeling guilty about the whole thing, I backed down off the rock.

We resumed our hike, and soon after we came to a small creek. Zenith decided we should work our way up it for a while. By the look of things, something else had been working its way up just ahead of us. A shallow hole had been scraped out of one bank; water was seeping into it. And flat rocks lay overturned along the stream's edge, their bottoms still glistening with water. Plainly, an animal was hunting for salamanders, insect larvae or other small prey. There were also wet splotches on rocks and on pebble bars. All the marks seemed larger than those a raccoon would leave with its delicate paws, though the outline was so indistinct it was impossible to know for sure if the animal we were following so closely was, as we suspected, a bear.

Several hundred yards farther along the muddy bank, we finally came across the clear tracks of a small bear leaving the stream and heading into the woods. At the same point there was a set of deer tracks going in the same direction. For a moment I wondered if the bear was stalking the deer. However, it was unlikely in this forest of plenty, where bears can usually eat their fill just from casual foraging, and stalking a deer takes a lot more time and trouble than the bears are ready to devote to the task. Maybe this bear was following a deer but more than likely it and the deer had simply left the stream at the same small break in foliage of the overgrown banks.

We left the stream bed ourselves at the next bend and as we resumed our walk through the forest I felt for the first time a spaciousness about me. We had reached deep into the cove, where ancient trees still grew. The bare trunks of basswoods, buckeyes and other trees reached up 40, 50, 60 feet before their huge limbs spread outward. Zenith pointed to a pile of fresh wood chips on the ground, nodded upward and said: "Woodpecker working on one of the big branches there."

I had been puzzled before he spoke. In more modest woods, woodpecker chips are usually found right at the base of a trunk. This pile was 25 feet away from the nearest tree. Or so I thought. I stopped and looked upward, long and hard; way above us a canopy of leaves covered the entire forest—as it had in Bartram's time. That canopy comprised a complete biological environment, connected to the ground by trunks and vines, but existing as a well-populated world of its own.

The trees here grew like huge candelabra—but designed to take light instead of give it. Above the leaves the sunlight was still intense on this late summer day, but as little as five to 10 per cent of it reached the forest floor; the rest was blocked by the leaves. Though the phenomenon occurs too slowly for me to actually observe, I knew that the leaves twist and turn, giving them the maximum benefit of sunshine.

A plant hormone called auxin is responsible for these leaf movements. Auxin in the cells of a leaf stalk concentrates on the shaded side of the leaf causing the cells to elongate. As the shaded side grows longer, the stalk slowly turns the leaf until the sunny side becomes the shaded side—at which point the movement reverses. In a potted plant the motion is apparent almost from day to day; in most of these giant deciduous trees the movement of the leaves occurs more gradually, and therefore less obviously. On the trees around me the leaves at the top were ranked, thin edge raised toward the sky, like louvers allowing the sunlight to filter down to lower layers of leaves.

An Ancient Mantle /67

Wood ferns (left and foreground) and the endemic herb Rugel's Indian plantain (in front of boulders) grow together near Andrews Bald.

Each of these layers, in an aerial universe like this one, supports different kinds of creatures. Only tough customers like crows and hawks and ingenious nest builders like Baltimore orioles make their homes high up in the canopy, exposed to the full force of wind and rain. The animals I like best—because I know them best, I guess—nest in the more sheltered levels. My favorite tenants of the middle zone are the squirrels, the most regular and diverting company a hiker can find in the Southern Appalachians. Their tightrope act along the branches never ceases to fascinate me. Occasionally they miss but even then their lightning reflexes and great physical resilience usually save them from any serious injury. In a fall, they will twist and then flatten themselves out like a spread-eagled skydiver to slow their descent.

They also have ingenious—and remarkably civilized—methods of solving their social problems. Once in a walk through tall oaks in the Nantahala Mountains of North Carolina, I was stopped by an angry squawk that came from a point way above me. In a moment I had picked up the squawker in my field glasses. It was a gray squirrel, its tail jerking gracelessly back and forth with no flow or whip to it. One moment it was on the left, then on the right.

All this business was what zoologists call a threat display, the type of thing known among us higher mammals as May Day or Armed Forces Day parades. The object of menace in this case was another squirrel several trees away. A ballet of mock violence was underway. The two squirrels would charge, head first, down the tree trunks to the ground, blast through the leaves to another tree, up again to make squawking noises and then back down again. They were careful to stay at least one tree away from each other, however. Sometimes the defending squirrel would stop dead on a branch to squawk, and twitch its tail faster and faster if the enemy approached. Bluster finally drove off the challenger. The winner and still-defending territorial champion gave a sort of chirring call, triumphant.

Though the gray squirrel is the one I've seen most in the Southern mountains, the flying squirrel is also widespread. It is nocturnal, however, and its acrobatic feats are seldom seen by man. That is a shame because those who have witnessed them report that the squirrel walks way out on a limb, 60 feet or so up in the air, gathers its feet together and then leaps into space, all four legs splayed. Folds of skin connect the hind and forelegs, creating a pair of semiwings. By moving its legs on one side or the other, the squirrel can control its angle, speed and di-

The red squirrel thrives in Southern Appalachian forests as far south as Georgia. Known locally as the mountain boomer for its repertoire of scolding chatter and other noises, this lively creature is marked by its red color and distinctive white underparts.

An Ancient Mantle /69

rection. It can maneuver in midair to avoid a branch and then continue its glide to land head up on the trunk of another tree as much as 150 feet away from its starting point. If the squirrel happens to be making an extended trip across the forest, it will climb up one tree, walk out on a high limb as far as it can go and then glide down to the next tree and so on. Dozens of these friendly squirrels may nest together, snuggled down on a bed of collected debris packed into a big tree hollow; individuals nest in smaller holes, such as those made and abandoned by woodpeckers. Arthur Stupka, retired naturalist for the Great Smoky Mountains National Park, told me that a park crew cutting down a dead chestnut once scared 26 of the little animals out of a communal winter hole high in the trunk.

I saw a flying squirrel in the wild myself just once—and, frankly, some of my friends insist it may not have been one. I was poking through some open woods in the Pisgah National Forest of North Carolina when I came across what looked like a fallen bird's nest. Thinking it was empty, I bent over and touched it and out burst a small dun-colored animal with a sparse-haired, flat tail. The animal disappeared into nearby brush before I could focus properly on it. When I looked down again, the nest was bulging with movement like a blanket thrown over puppies. I knew there were young inside so I left quickly, hoping I had not disturbed the mother so much that she would not return. Later, a zoologist told me that what I had seen was probably a chipmunk, because flying squirrels do not nest on the ground. I know what a chipmunk looks like, though, and the animal that fled did not appear to be one. I still think it was a flying squirrel.

Zenith had been silent for a long time. We had passed dozens of tulip trees in our walk, but none of them was Zenith's tree. Suddenly he gave a sharp shout and pointed. Way up on the slope I spied a massive dark gray trunk, hulking in the dappled sunlight.

We scrambled up the mountainside, and only when we were right alongside the tree did I get the full sense of how enormous it really was. I held one end of Zenith's measuring tape while he worked his way around the trunk, disappeared from view and then reappeared on the other side. At chest height, the tulip tree measured 23 feet 1 inch around, or about seven feet through. It was probably 100 feet or more in height and for most of that distance the trunk swept straight up, clear of branches. I judged its age to be more than 300 years.

Zenith thumped on the dark, furrowed bark and I was startled by the dull, hollow sound. He told me to look over on the other side. There was an opening in the trunk at ground level just big enough for me to crawl inside. In old tulip trees such openings are common; they are caused by fungi that enter a wound and generate decay in the heartwood. They arouse in me a feeling of mystery—the mystery of childhood explorations for woodland spirits.

I squirmed inside and I found myself in a roughly circular chamber so wide that, with arms extended, I couldn't quite touch the opposite walls. The chamber went up farther than the beam of my pocket flashlight could reach. Wood beetles, carpenter ants or termites had carved the walls into intricate trenches and crenelations, so deeply sculpted that the whole effect was of hanging draperies colored a rich, reddish brown. The room was perfectly dry, with the clean smell of a carpentry shop rather than with the dank odor of decay. Dry rot, a fungus that thrives in wood containing little moisture, seemed to have helped the insects eat out the tree's heart. My feet sank into the soft, springy floor, as if into a pile of dry sawdust.

It occurred to me that the room would make a perfect shelter for larger animals, perhaps bears or bobcats. Even humans had sheltered in such places during the frontier days. An 18th Century surveyor-general in North Carolina reported that "a lusty Man had his Bed and Household Furniture" moved into a tulip tree while he built his house.

When I crawled outside, Zenith and I stood for a moment, each thinking his own thoughts about this tree and the forest around it. For Zenith there was great satisfaction in finding his old friend still standing, a reaffirmation of kinship with the forest he had known since earliest childhood. To me there was some of the same, though this was my first time in this particular patch of woods. And I had another feeling, at once moving and companionable. This tree was more than three centuries old. It had been here when Bartram rambled through the Southern Appalachians, part of the forest that he had marveled at then and that I could marvel at now. A hundred years from now, with good fortune, it might still be here. And I hoped someone, way off then, would see the woods as the three of us have seen it—Bartram, Zenith and I.

NATURE WALK / In Linville Gorge

PHOTOGRAPHS BY ROBERT WALCH

At the very edge of the Blue Ridge, where the mountains begin to ease down into the foothills of North Carolina's Piedmont country, is a place called Linville Gorge in Pisgah National Forest. I've wanted to visit it ever since I heard the name. I am a sucker for gorges—it is a weakness probably dating back to early exposure to Samuel Taylor Coleridge's lines "deep romantic chasm . . . with ceaseless turmoil seething."

This particular chasm was originally opened eons ago by the progenitor of the Linville River, which is still slowly cutting deeper into the valley as it threads its way south to join the Catawba River; the gorge is now 1,700 feet deep. I visited it for the first time at the very beginning of May, that time of year when soft rains and the delicate green of new leaves give the North Carolina countryside an undersea look. With me was photographer Bob Walch, who wanted to capture just this look of misty green, tingeing the black of the branches and setting in relief the more somber green of the spruces and hemlocks.

The weather was unsettled on the morning Bob and I set out. Bright sun alternated with cloud cover that diffused the light. We were to begin our journey through the 12-mile gorge at Linville Falls. Recent rains had so swollen the river that we could hear the falls from a forest path several hundred yards away. When we reached them, we found a crashing 90-foot tumult of white water. We stood on a rock outcropping and watched the water seethe past in an endless roar.

Below us lay the gorge itself, and in it, roiling off into the distance, the river ran between steep banks covered with red spruce and yellow birch not yet in full leaf. On the right bank, just where the river disappeared around a bend, was a small heath bald. From our vantage point it looked like an inviting clearing in the woods, but I knew that its tangled rhododendrons would be harder to get through than the forest itself. I was glad that our path—as far as I could tell from the map—would lead us around that obstacle.

We left the falls and started into the woods. On the forest floor we saw winterberry, a tiny, crawling member of the heath family, and a few painted trilliums, the scarlet blazes on their petals making neat triangles at the flowers' centers. But there was little other undergrowth.

We were in a stand of hemlock

THE GORGE BELOW LINVILLE FALLS

that seemed to go on forever. I learned later from a forest ranger that this grove, comprising some 100 acres, is one of the largest virgin hemlock stands in the East. As we walked through it the stillness was overwhelming and the shade so deep that only a few plants seemed to be able to thrive in it.

A PAINTED TRILLIUM

Below the falls, the trail detoured temporarily away from the river. The hemlocks became mixed with rhododendrons and yellow birches —a mixture typically found on such north-facing slopes in Southern Appalachian coves or in similarly sheltered locations. The trail was still slick underfoot, a reminder of the rains that drench the Blue Ridge Mountains so regularly. Drops of water from condensation and the previous evening's downpour hung on the leaves, weighing down some

74/ **In Linville Gorge**

A HEMLOCK GROVE

of the branches so that they hung over the trail.

But the springtime dampness set the hemlock forest off to its best advantage. Lichens, whose colors would have been drab and dusty in dry times, now shone brightly on the trees—silver and yellow and green, almost as if they were lighted by some interior glow.

An Immature Fungus

We came upon a fungus called ganoderma, which resembled bulbous white teeth with stained roots, popping improbably out of the wood of a dying tree. If I hadn't observed a ganoderma colony near my house over a full growing season some years before, I wouldn't have had any idea what these curious growths were. Young ganoderma bodies bear little more resemblance to mature ones than a caterpillar does to a butterfly. These unusual protuberances would eventually turn into shelflike fungi eight inches or more across, colored a deep blood red. The surface, now dull and soft, would become hard and as shiny as if it had been shellacked.

The next curiosity we happened upon was a rock covered with bluish-gray rock tripe, a species of lichen that is black or deep chocolate brown when dry. Like the immature ganoderma these large, flat lichens are edible—but barely so. Oliver P. Medsger in *Edible Wild Plants* describes the delights of rock tripe with bridled enthusiasm: "They are somewhat mucilaginous and... they are almost tasteless; at least, the taste is not pleasing. I am quite con-

LICHENS ON A TREE TRUNK

GANODERMA FUNGUS

ROCK TRIPE

A TRANQUIL VIEW FROM RIVERSIDE

vinced that they would be much better cooked with meat or other tasty food."

So I did not bother to collect a big mess of rock tripe for supper. Instead, I contented myself with tearing off a leathery strip and nibbling at its edge. The stuff was, as advertised, tasteless.

A POLYGYRID SNAIL

The trail finally led us down to the river, here 40 feet wide and placid after its constricted and violent tumble over the falls. The water was yellowish green in color. From a distance the trees on the other side seemed luminous where the sun hit their first unfolding leaves. When we sat down to enjoy the view, we spotted the first fauna of the expedition: a snail. It was passing over fallen twigs and leaves imperturbably and at an almost imperceptible pace. The snail seemed somehow bright and alert, probably because of its shiny little bulbs of eyes on top of its retractable tentacles. Quite possibly as a result of my early and frequent exposure to science-fiction comic books, I decided that the snail, seen close up like this, gave a fair imitation of a Martian.

A Miracle of Motion

Bob then spotted another equally bizarre creature: a harmless, vegetarian millipede crawling over a

A MILLIPEDE

stone. Its multitude of legs (not a thousand, as the name suggests, but surely hundreds) were arranged as two fringes running down either side of a shiny segmented body, with waves of movement passing rhythmically down them like the ruffles made in meadow grass by the wind. Next to the everyday miracle of a millipede in normal motion, a concert pianist running through his arpeggios is all thumbs.

After leaving the river, we discovered that hiking in Linville Gorge means covering almost twice as much ground as the length of the gorge itself. You simply can't walk

TUFTS OF PANIC GRASS

in a straight line down the river's edge; steep banks turn here and there into cliff faces of sheer rock that jut out into the river. Thus we had only a brief walk along the river before we found that the trail detoured straight up (or what felt like straight up) a hillside so steep we could progress only by grabbing handholds on trees, shrubs and exposed roots. We scrambled up the gorge's walls, past great overhangs of various metamorphic rocks, predominant among them mica schist and arkose gneiss.

As solid and inhospitable as the rock walls appeared, the process that would eventually reduce them to dust and soil had already started. Enough airborne or waterborne debris had settled in the cracks to provide a foothold for panic grass —the name panic being derived from its genus name Panicum—mosses and other small plants, whose roots would gradually pry into the tiniest

CRACKS IN A ROCK FACE

crevices and help crumble the rock.

Here and there as we climbed we came across some newly flowering shrubs. Most curious were those of a shrub called horse sugar, or sweetleaf, whose stemless blooms burst directly out of the twigs. The flowers give off a markedly sweet odor, and the leaves, equally sweet to the taste, are said to be a great favorite of horses.

An Old Home Remedy

Nearby was a sassafras in bloom; its yellowish blossoms were so inconspicuous that I wouldn't have recognized them except for the small leaves just coming out along the branches. But sassafras makes identification easy for even the most amateur botanists. There are male and female flowers, with yellow antler-like stamens protruding from the stem of the male plant. Some species of sassafras even bear leaves of three entirely different shapes, often on the same twig. One type is formed like a mitten; the second like a mitten with thumbs on either side; the third like an oval leaf. Sassafras roots are still used in perfumery and for flavoring—notably of root beer. But their medicinal value—once so esteemed as a remedy for general ailments that they commanded £336 per ton in England at the opening of the 17th Century—has proved upon scientific investigation to be more psychological than real.

Of no particular historical value but of great beauty were the crested dwarf irises we came across along this path; their blue petals were marked with orange almost as if tiny

HORSE-SUGAR BLOSSOMS

MALE SASSAFRAS FLOWERS

flames were licking out from inside.

When our climbing ended and the trail leveled out, we were far above the stream and across the gorge from a rock formation called Babel Tower Rock, which rears up in a horseshoe bend in the river. We were almost on a level with the top of Babel Tower Rock, but to reach it would have meant climbing all the way down into the gorge and up again. So we headed down a steep trail instead, back toward the floor of the ravine once more.

On this narrow section of the river, the metamorphic rocks on the gorge bed erupted through the water in a gallery of fantastically sculptured shapes. Carved by thousands of years of running water, the gray boulders broke the river up into tiny rapids and waterfalls. We picked our way downstream, hopping from one to another of the enormous, weath-

CRESTED DWARF IRIS

A NARROW STRETCH OF THE RIVER

ered rocks that encumbered the stream bed.

The Linville has the reputation of being a fine trout stream, but we didn't spot any fish in the shallow water near shore. Once, however, we saw a half dozen small salamanders moving slowly about on the bottom of a basin in the bedrock, separated from the main stream but still full from recent rains.

In still patches near the bank, water striders raced about seemingly at random, sustained by the thin skin of surface tension on the water. Actually their dashes were probably not random, but directed at insects, too small for us to see, that had fallen onto the river's surface.

Wherever the trail led us away from the streamside and into the woods, we found ourselves walking through carpets of spring flowers dappled by the sun. Overhead the leaves of maple, oak and birch trees, barely unfolding from their buds, let far more light penetrate to the forest floor than they would later in the summer. Seizing their brief season in the sun, tiny bluets spangled the woods with four-pointed blue-white stars, making a snowy background for the green leaves of violets and wild geraniums. I stooped to pick a few violet leaves to chew on as I walked along. Particularly when new and tender, they make a fine salad ingredient.

The seedlings of touch-me-not, their stems topped by half-inch-long leaves rectangular in shape but with rounded edges, were just coming up through the dead leaves. They are also supposed to be edible. I've never tasted them, but I have used the plant's juice with some success as a treatment for poison-ivy rash. The touch-me-not is a plant of many peculiar properties. Its waxy leaves are waterproof, so that during a shower, raindrops stand on them in tiny beads—which gives the plant its other common name, jewelweed.

Touch-me-not is spindly and frail in appearance, with a watery, light-orange sap—and yet it grows higher than a person's waist by the end of summer. There is some evidence that the plant's sap is useful not only against poison ivy, but may also have some effect in ameliorating fungus disorders of the skin. Early autumn is when the touch-me-not merits its name: if you brush against the plants, the pods burst open with an audible pop, and the seeds fly several feet. In the absence of human assistance, the plant distributes its seeds whenever an animal, insect or breeze rustles its stalks.

The afternoon was well along when we stopped for a good rest in anticipation of a steep, unrelieved climb of some 1,200 feet that the map indicated ahead of us. It would lead us out of the gorge entirely and to the top of the ridgeline that separated it from the next valley.

Disturber of the Peace

The summertime murmuring of insects had not yet started, and the woods were absolutely still as we lay resting on the ground. Then suddenly came the call of a flicker, and the hammering of its beak as the woodpecker worked away at a tree, above us somewhere and unseen. It was as good an alarm clock as any, and so we heaved ourselves upright and began the assault.

The climb was every bit as steep as it had appeared to be on the map. The only consolation was that the way was shady, because the trail led us through evergreen hemlocks and rhododendrons and along the banks of a small stream, which ran

A WATER STRIDER

BLUETS

A TOUCH-ME-NOT SHOOT AMONG VIOLET LEAVES

down the side of the gorge to empty into the river at the bottom. The rhododendron appears throughout the Appalachian range, but it is only here in the southern section that it outgrows the shrub category and becomes a tree. Though these huge rhododendrons gave shade, it was too early for them to be in bloom. We had seen a few laurel blossoms along the river, but the big show would come later on.

Soon we arrived at a spot that offered a view across the gorge, and I used my field glasses to examine more closely what I had thought were dogwoods blossoming partway up the opposite bank. They turned out to be silver bells—loose sprays of white flowers standing out against the pale green of the first foliage. Men have introduced the silver bell tree well to the north now, but it thrives best in its original Southern home, sometimes reaching a height of 100 feet in the fertile Southern Appalachian coves.

About halfway through our climb we came upon an undersized waterfall, where the stream ran over a ledge and dropped six or eight feet into a small pool. We stopped to rest a while and to drink the clear, cold water. Trickling out of crevices in the rock, the stream had made niches of coolness and moisture here and there along the ledge—little habitats suitable for mosses and their close botanical cousins, liverworts. On the drier forest floor, back from the stream, we saw showy orchises—small terrestrial orchids with pastel pink-and-white flowers that stood

In Linville Gorge /83

out strikingly against the dark green of the plants' broad, straplike leaves. Near the orchises, fiddleheads of the intermediate wood fern were just unfolding. They looked like bishops' crosiers of deep, succulent green.

Once we had left the small waterfall, it became noticeable that there was less and less feathery green in the woods, more and more black or gray. We had gained enough altitude to have walked back a few days toward winter; at this height, spring would lag a few days behind its schedule down in the more protected, warmer gorge. When we finally topped out, reaching the dirt road that ran along the spine of the ridge we had been climbing, we noticed that the trees were barely out of their bud stage.

A Scenic Reward

The rest of our hike was easy—a level stroll along the edge of the gorge to Wiseman's View, a magnificent overlook whose vista includes Hawksbill Mountain nearly straight across the gorge, Tablerock Mountain to the southeast, Brown Mountain lying farther east in the gap between the two mountains, and the Linville River's twisting path as it continues southward.

While Bob recorded with his camera the changing lights and shadows in the valley as the day faded, I stopped to examine a tulip-tree sapling whose leaves, burgeoning from their leaf bracts, looked almost like tiny replicas of a police badge. To me the leaves of the tulip tree are the most elegant of any tree I know. And these miniature ones, perfectly

A SYLVAN WATERFALL

MOSSES AND LIVERWORTS IN A LEDGE

A SHOWY ORCHIS

INTERMEDIATE WOOD FERN

FLOWERING MOUNTAIN MYRTLE

formed and of the freshest pale green, were like little jewels. But the majority of the trees on the cool, north-facing slopes of the gorge were hemlocks, with an understory of rhododendrons. The trees across the river were oaks mixed with white pines and alder bushes overhanging the water—a typical assemblage of species found in the warmer, drier southern exposures of the Southern Appalachians. I sat as near the cliff's edge as I dared, amid glossy-leafed mountain myrtle. This heath plant grows most commonly in the Southern Appalachian balds, but can also be found clinging to exposed rocks and sprouting from crevices. With its white blossoms accented by red stamens and glossy evergreen leaves it is very like its close relative, the alpine azalea, which is seen in the White Mountains of New England. Growing in dense beds from 15 to 20 inches tall, the flowers form a starry mat when they are at their peak during June. On this May day the pink-white buds seemed about to pop open. I admired the play of late afternoon light on these hardy little plants, and wondered about a different variety of natural lighting effects of which I had heard. These are the mysterious Brown Mountain lights, named for the mountain where they occur. It was too early in the day to see the lights, I knew, and it was hardly worth waiting until after dark on the off chance that they might appear. United States Forest Officer C. W. Smith had told me earlier that he had searched many years for the lights and had just about concluded that they were mythical when at last he spotted them one night, in the gap directly east of my lookout at Wiseman's View, between Hawksbill and Tablerock mountains. "One would go on for a few seconds," Smith had said, "and then die down, and then others would light up far away somewhere, and fade again."

The glowing lights have been well authenticated, but both the rarity and brevity of their appearance have made it impossible for scientists to figure out just what it is that causes them. Phosphorescence? Some sort of electrical activity in the atmosphere? Whatever natural explanation the lights may turn out to have, they will nonetheless continue to form part of the magic of this hazy Southern valley.

In Linville Gorge

PANORAMA SOUTH FROM WISEMAN'S VIEW

3/ The Forest Floor

For three hundred and fifty million years roots have been thrusting in these rocks, leaves have been falling upon other fallen leaves, sweetening the soil.

RODERICK PEATTIE/ THE GREAT SMOKIES AND THE BLUE RIDGE

When I was a boy wandering the woods I used to think how handy it would be if a light pinpointed the place where each animal lay hidden from me. I had in mind a system something like the one in the English poet Coleridge's "The Rime of the Ancient Mariner"—seraph-creatures of light to mark each spot. If I turned over the stone under this faint violet nebula over here I would be rewarded by the sight of a tiny red and black and gray milk snake, fresh out of its egg and gleaming bright as enamel. That greenish glow a little farther up the hill, on the other hand, would signal a hidden nest of mice, where half-grown babies squirmed in a companionable huddle of white-and-cinnamon fur.

Lacking such a system, I was compelled to leave quite a mess behind me as I poked around in the forest. As curious as a bear, I couldn't stand to leave a strip of bark or a log or a rock unturned. In the process I made a series of observations that seemed to hold true for reasons I learned only when I reached adulthood. Nothing very interesting would be found under a piece of oak bark (too acid for many organisms, I later discovered); if ants were under a rock, not much else would be (the ants themselves, with their formidable bites, see to that); stones in swampy ground would not be worth turning over (they settle in so tightly that little living space is left).

But under just the right slabs of shale or rotting logs, in well-drained ground, I might find almost anything: millipedes, centipedes, pill bugs, salamanders, snakes, all kinds of things worth seeing. And more fascinating still were the traces left behind by creatures I did *not* see. Under nearly every stone would be some evidence of life—portions of passages suddenly unroofed, shed snake skins or abandoned mouse nests. All these traces argued the presence of an enormous, thriving community beneath my feet.

We lived in the foothills of Virginia's Blue Ridge when I was in my teens. By then I had awakened to the fact that nobody was going to put out signal lanterns on top of Toad Hall for me, or shrink me down to rabbit size like Alice. To get a close look at the inhabitants of the forest floor I would have to depend on luck, which came along only at very long intervals, or on patience, which I had plenty of.

One notable stroke of luck occurred when a man who did some plowing for us turned up a big brown snake. It was heavy bodied, as thick through as the handle of a shovel and about a yard long. At that age I thought I knew every kind of snake in Virginia by sight, but I hadn't a clue to this one, a dull reddish brown without any pattern. It was a mole snake, my books finally told me, one of the family of king snakes, underground rodent eaters, that rarely sees the light of day. Weird. How many more of them—and their prey—were down there? If my childhood dream system had come true, would the whole field be lit up like a pinball machine?

Patience delivered more to me. I used to sit in the woods for hours, waiting for things to come out. In spring or early fall when the bugs were not too bad, I would take up a vigil and watch for as long as I felt like keeping still. Most often I saw chipmunks, which lead such public lives above ground that I quickly lost interest in their surface scurrying. What I really wanted to see was the underground habitat a chipmunk excavates a yard below the surface.

Over the chipmunk's four- or five-year life span, I had read, it may dig up to 30 feet of tunnels radiating out from a main room. The big chamber, if I could only see one, would be perhaps a foot high and a foot wide, with a bed of grass or leaves and a passage leading down to a separate little toilet room at a lower level. This was the kind of elaborate layout Mr. Badger had in Kenneth Grahame's *The Wind in the Willows,* and it would have been worth seeing.

Though mildly frustrated by my inability to explore the underground realm of the chipmunk, I felt privileged in countless other ways, for the woods I wandered offered unending opportunities for the curious. The floor of any deciduous forest teems with life, and since the Southern Ap-

The undergrowth of this high-altitude spruce forest on Clingmans Dome is limited to herbs and wood ferns, in large part because the composition of the soil and decaying conifer needles render the forest floor too acidic for other flora. Although plant-sustaining moisture increases with the altitude, temperatures above 5,000 feet are not high enough to support vegetation common to the lower elevations.

The Forest Floor /89

palachians are covered with a deciduous forest unmatched in its diversity by any in North America, it follows that the floor life is correspondingly varied. Had I lived in a region dominated by coniferous forests, my interest might have flagged early: fallen conifer needles create such acid soil conditions that little understory plant life can take hold; and without plants to attract them, animals are scarce. But in the Southern Appalachians, whose woodlands, valleys and streams harbor a wide assortment of life, the rich soil is the fundament of a complicated pyramidal food chain—much of it far too small to be seen even with luck or patience, but nonetheless marvelous to contemplate.

The floor that generates this complex life system—and is indeed part of it—is made up of several layers of earth. The top layers, where virtually all the action is, consist of rich humus: the partially decomposed remains of plants and animals. Just below are the leached layers, where dissolved organic and mineral matter have filtered downward. Farther down, there are the so-called enriched layers, where materials percolated from above have reached maximum accumulation. Next to last is weathered rock, the disintegrating parent material of the soil, which helps determine its composition, thickness and fertility; and, at the very bottom, unweathered rock.

Stepping on the spongy upper strata of forest soil, moist, deep and rich, is something like sinking into a feather bed. There is an elastic springiness to it, as if millions of unseen creatures underfoot were heaving back up to get the weight off their backs. Actually, the sponginess comes from the fact that the soil is far from solid, and hardly ever completely dry. As little as 40 per cent of it may be bits of mineral, vegetable or animal matter. The rest consists of pockets of air—or water, which is absorbed downward after a rainfall and held in the tiny interstices between soil grains. In a dry spell, when the top of the surface soil layer feels completely parched, at various depths every soil particle remains coated with a thin film of water, and water in vapor form will still be present in the air between the soil grains in some layers. Thus even in a drought, there is enough nourishing moisture both for plants with extensive root systems and for the microscopic life that dominates the humus layers and is such an integral part of it.

Humus is a fertile mineral and organic stew, in which part of the organic matter is in the process of decay and part is very much alive. Tree and plant roots are obvious elements of living plant matter. Generally less obvious are the fungi, so many of which are far too infinitesimal in size to be seen, but whose role in the food chain is one of vital importance: they feed on plant and animal matter, both dead and alive, and in turn provide nourishment for small animals and trees. Now and then fungi thrust parts of themselves above the surface, and balloon up into shapes large enough to be examined. Most common are the mushrooms, which seem to appear from nowhere. Overnight, a fallen log or patch of moss will be covered with them, and then they will retreat almost as fast into the earth from which they sprang.

On a day in August, when I was camped with my family on top of Roanoke Mountain in southern Virginia, I saw the best fungus display of my life. One of my sons came up to me holding a species called Caesar's mushroom, the size of a pie plate, brick red on top and yellow on the bottom. He said there were mushrooms all over the woods, and we went out to have a look. He was right: they were all around, by the hundreds and the thousands. Experts have catalogued about 2,000 species on the forest floor of the Southern Appalachians, although nothing like that many will ever be in view at once. Still, we found a dozen or more different species within 100 yards of where we had camped.

In one little cove, for example, stood a clavaria, its yellow branches resembling coral, and a big clump of oakhare—locally called hen-of-the-woods—which also looks something like coral. The most prominent fungi of all, however, were the so-called milky mushrooms, which exude a milky or colored juice, and a dozen kinds of boletes—large specimens with caps of red, tan, yellow, pink and brown. Back near camp we found a good-sized stand of a deadly species appropriately named destroying angel. Most of them were pure white. They looked as if they would be one of the best mushrooms in the woods to eat, but in fact they are among the deadliest, killing violently. I once read a doctor's report on the deaths of a group of people who had eaten a stew containing them, and a certain sentence from that report has always stayed in my mind: "Annie M., the seven-year-old child, was the first to be relieved by death." Even if Annie had escaped immediate death, she might well have suffered irreparable liver damage.

Those ghostly destroying angels and all the other mushrooms we saw in the woods that day were only the fruiting part of the fungi, that is, the part that carries the spores. For the mushroom is to the whole fungus organism as the apple is to the tree. The real body of the plant is a network of tiny threadlike tubes called hyphae, which spread throughout the soil of the forest floor in incredible profusion. There may be up to two *miles* of them laced through a single ounce of soil. They are the main agents in the decomposition of wood and leaves, which they break down chemically for food. Without the hyphae, fallen leaves, twigs, branches and tree trunks would eventually turn the forest into a brush pile. With the hyphae, however, the forest's sheddings are converted into softer stuff, rotted material that gradually becomes part of the humus and in the process is partly eaten by soil-dwelling creatures.

Fungi play another crucial role in the forest. Mushroom hunters have long known that certain varieties are found near certain trees. Fly agarics and rough-stemmed boletes, for example, are usually found close to birch trees. The reason for this is that these fungi enter into mutual-benefit arrangements with the roots. Some investigators suspect that virtually all forest trees, in fact, benefit from such arrangements, which are known as mycorhizal relationships. The fungi act in effect as extensions of the tree's roots, bringing in increased supplies of mineral salts and other nutrients. The fungi, in turn, benefit from the shade, which helps them to retain moisture.

One step above the fungi on the chain are bacteria—tiny creatures that also live in and off the soil, and repay their debt by helping to form new soil. They, like the fungi's hyphae, are too small to examine with the unaided eye; but magnified, many of them appear in shapes so bizarre that they have the look of immigrants from another planet. Some have legs and segments like insects, some are as shapeless as leeches; some appear to be nothing more than threads. Often they dine on plant life, both dead and alive, including fungi. Just as often they dine on each other, biting, piercing and even garroting each other in a never-ending quest for food. A single gram (about 1/30 of an ounce) of fertile soil can contain more than one billion bacteria; 250,000 of them could fit on the space covered by a printed period. My mind boggles at the thought. It reels even more at the knowledge that each bacterium, reproducing under ideal conditions, could cover a football field with about a foot-thick layer of its descendants in 24 hours. Since no one has ever seen a football field in such an extraordinary fix, it is plain that something is keeping conditions for the bacteria less than ideal.

And indeed something is; several things, each a deadly enemy of the bacteria. One group of opponents are the indeterminate forms, neither flora nor fauna but in-between organisms called actinomycetes, which create the "earthy" smell of soil. These bear some relation to fungi and some to bacteria, but are neither. Instead they compete with bacteria for organic residues. The competition is not altogether fair, since the ac-

The mushrooms and other fungi on the following pages are all found in the moist hardwood forests of the Southern Appalachians. Of the 12, only the jack o'lantern is poisonous; but few are particularly palatable. They perform an essential function, however. Fungi—plants without chlorophyll—are important garbage recyclers of the forest. They secrete enzymes that aid in the breakdown and decomposition of plant and animal matter, thus providing nourishment for themselves and other organisms.

The Forest Floor /93

BERKELEY'S POLYPORE

A VARIETY OF CAESAR'S MUSHROOM

ONE OF THE LEPIOTA MUSHROOMS

BRICK-TOP MUSHROOM

94/

COKER'S AMANITA MUSHROOM

CHANTERELLE HYGROPHORUS MUSHROOM

JACK O'LANTERN MUSHROOM

RETICULATE-STEMMED BOLETE

The Forest Floor /95

LYCOGALA EPIDENDRUM SLIME MOLD

BROAD-GILLED COLLYBIA MUSHROOM

CHICKEN MUSHROOM

WITCH'S BUTTER JELLY FUNGUS

tinomycetes generate and exude substances that inhibit the growth of bacteria. These substances—streptomycin is one—are called antibiotics. Within the forest floor, they give the actinomycetes an edge at meal times. In the world of humans, they form the bases for medicines that combat such diseases as strep throat and pneumonia.

Microscopic single-celled animals called protozoa are also responsible for holding the bacteria in check. Protozoa are a great deal bigger than bacteria, so big that a mere 10,000 to 100,000 of them are able to crowd into that same gram of soil. They move about in the soil's subsurface water film or vapor, hunting down bacteria. Whenever their subterranean environment dries out to such a degree that bacteria become scarce, the protozoa simply grow hard coatings around themselves and wait for rain. Protozoa thus encysted have been known to survive in dry soil for half a century.

Protozoa are pretty good reproducers themselves, dividing twice a day or more. Like bacteria, protozoa might pose a population problem—if it were not for soil nematodes, minute unsegmented worms that resemble bits of fine thread. These creatures occupy the top two inches of the soil, sometimes as many as 20 million to the square yard, consuming both protozoa and vegetable matter.

A nematode, in turn, may literally be lassoed by a fungus. One fungus, the *Dactylella doedycoides*, possesses hyphae with spurs running off to the sides, each spur tipped by a loop. The loops swell, like the arm wrappings into which doctors pump air to gauge blood pressure, whenever an unsuspecting nematode swims through. The loop then constricts, strangling the nematode around the midriff. Prongs then appear on the loop, penetrate the nematode and digest it.

Even if the nematode should escape the fungus, it risks being sucked up like a piece of spaghetti by another of the ravenous, soil-dwelling rivals, the omnivorous springtail. Springtails—primitive wingless insects —are still pretty small, but a few kinds are more than a quarter of an inch long. They have six abdominal segments (instead of the 11 of more advanced insects), and a projection sticking down from the belly that helps to stake them in place and may be useful to absorb water. Some species, venturesome cousins that spend a fair portion of their time on the surface of the forest floor, also have a tail that curves down under the abdomen, where it is locked into place with a sort of catch. When the springtail trips the catch, the tail flips loose and catapults the creature into the air and away from the many bigger insects that chase

A meadow vole shrinks defensively into its burrow in the glare of a photographer's flash. Prey to nearly every carnivore—mammal, bird or reptile—in the Southern Appalachian woodlands, the vole seldom lives more than a year, but maintains its species population with a phenomenal reproductive capacity: it can have as many as 17 litters in one year.

it. A few types of springtails exude their distasteful or even toxic blood through small pores when threatened. One way or another springtails survive well enough so that they can even manage a population explosion now and then.

Springtails represent the beginning of the visible world in the food chain, though you have to look mighty hard to see them. But then, you have to look mighty hard to see most of the interesting things in the forest. For example, did you ever pull apart a rotted log to find out what was happening inside? I have. That I can pull one apart at all, of course, means that a succession of other animals have had at the log before me. First come various shallow-boring grubs (which rank a little above springtails in the chain). They are succeeded by such deep borers as sawyer-beetle larvae, powder-post beetles and termites.

Water seeps into the tunnels, making the wood damp enough for fungi to penetrate and soften it. Bacteria, fungus-eating beetles and mites work on it further. Then something disruptive like a bear or myself comes along and knocks it apart. Or the log simply settles by itself into the soil, surrounded by dead leaves and twigs. Pill bugs, millipedes and earthworms chew up tiny pieces, making it even smaller. Thereby they increase the surface area available for bacteria to work on—and thereby, too, they help to reduce the log until it returns to the soil from which it had sprung many decades before as a seedling to grow into a mature tree.

Even during its strongest years of life, that tree and its neighbors were helping to build the soil by depositing a ton or more of dead leaves on every acre of forest each year. As the leaves crumble, night crawlers pull broken-up bits of them back into their burrows and coat the fragments with a substance that helps decompose them so that the worm can swallow and digest them. Slugs and snails help the job along. So do the vegetarian species of nematodes and springtails, swarming and struggling by the uncountable billions through the soil. Even in winter the process goes on with the fungi, bacteria, actinomycetes, protozoa, springtails and the rest grinding and dissolving away at the forest litter—and each other—insulated by snow from the freezing temperatures above. Little by little the deciduous forest, in the circular pattern of its existence, piles up fertile black humus, both nourishing the myriad life within it and being sustained and re-created by that life.

Though I would give anything to witness it all, I have learned to content myself with the life of the forest as played out by creatures big enough for me to see, both in the soil and above it. The struggle for existence aboveground is no less greedy and murderous; the mayhem is simply more visible. One night, camping in some luxury at a site at the foot of Lance Mountain in Pisgah National Forest, just south of Asheville, North Carolina, I was sitting outside my tent after dark, reading by the light of a propane lantern. The brilliant, hissing flame made a sort of lighted arena of the ground around my camp chair, and it quickly attracted all sorts of insects. Pretty soon I was paying more attention to the scene below me than to my book.

The aggressors were a large American toad and a hunting spider up on skinny legs like a wolfhound. All around them were crawling and flying insects beyond counting. The toad seemed to be too stimulated by the profusion of prey to sort out the impulses its eyes were passing back to its brain. It would hop one way and sit for a moment, then hop another way, like a beanbag heaving briefly to life. Now and then its eyes would make the right connection with its central nervous system so that a signal would be sent to the muscles controlling its sticky tongue. Then zap! The tongue, lumpy and formless, would shoot out to seize—or more often to miss—an insect from the air.

The hunting spider, meanwhile, tore back and forth in short dashes, and half the time nothing would be there when it arrived. It would stop and wait, menacing but inefficient, with prey buzzing everywhere within easy reach. Then the spider would race off a foot or so in another direction. Now and then it caught small things and ate them, but most of the time, like the hapless toad, it missed.

The insects swirled and swarmed and zoomed, making great, batty loops in the air as they responded to the imperatives of their circuitry. They made no effort to keep away from the toad and gave no sign of knowing there was a toad around, or even what a toad was. The toad and the spider, meanwhile, followed the dictates of their own overloaded circuitries. In this mathematical chaos two lines would intersect once in a while, and at that random instant something would die.

The relatively soft-bodied insects among these airborne victims seemed to have no defense or survival mechanism beyond sheer weight of numbers. And indeed, as I have since learned, they survive as a species not by cunning or speed or skill, but simply by breeding faster than the opposition can eat them. The larger invertebrates of the forest floor, on the other hand, take steps to ensure individual survival. In their world nearly everything wears armor—bands or wrappings of a hornlike material called chitin, which, in combination with protein, forms their external skeleton. The centipede has a poisonous bite as well as a chitinous exterior. In addition, if an enemy manages to grab a centipede by the leg, that leg will come off with no great damage to the victim. Moreover, the leg will continue to quiver, giving the predator the impression there is still a functioning centipede on the other end.

Color sometimes serves as an additional element of defense. Red and yellow are often signals to would-be predators that the bearer is venomous or unpalatable. Both colors are borne by some poisonous millipedes. Higher in the food chain, the same colors are used by two harmless burrowing snakes found in the Southern Appalachians—the scarlet snake and the scarlet king snake. Both reptiles somewhat resemble the venomous coral snake seen hereabouts, and perhaps for that reason hawks, skunks and foxes, which would find either a tasty dish, tend to leave them alone. By and large, however, snakes do not rely on brilliant color as a warning. On the contrary, those in the Southern Appalachian wilderness tend to have subtle coloration, which serves as camouflage—and very successful camouflage at that.

I have walked for days in these mountains without seeing a snake, and I am constantly on the lookout for them. Unlike other carnivores, snakes are cold blooded with no internal furnaces to keep stoked; they rely instead on solar heating. This means that they can survive on proportionately less food than is possible for warm-blooded meat eaters. And since they need do little foraging, they therefore spend a lot of their time lying still—and unnoticed—or in hiding. When they do come across food, though, they stuff themselves like sausages. One summer, in the Blue Ridge Mountains of Virginia just north of the North Carolina line, I caught a black rat snake that, in its fright, disgorged seven nearly grown mice. With such a meal inside, the reptile could have gone a month without eating again, and much longer in winter, when the relative lack of warmth makes all the region's snakes quiescent.

A snake rarely disgorges its stomach as the rat snake did for me. When one does so, a combination of instinct (to make itself lighter and thus able to move faster) and fear causes the spasmodic muscle reflex that triggers the evacuation. More often, to learn what a snake has or has not eaten recently, the snake must be killed and cut open. Left to its own devices, a snake hangs onto its dinner for as long as the digestive process takes, and its slow metabolic rate enables it to wait for its next meal even when it has completely digested the last one.

The smallest of the warm-blooded carnivorous mammals of the forest have no such staying power. I read once that a shrew in a cage with two others its own size ate both its cellmates within eight hours. Granted, the situation was abnormal: three high-strung ferocious shrews in a cage that was probably too small for them. Still, if you were to translate this achievement into the proportion of a man my size, the man would have to knock back 340 pounds of food in the course of a day. Normally, however, shrews are not cannibals. Beetles, fly larvae, crickets, mice, moths, grasshoppers, butterflies, worms, snails, lizards and salamanders are all part of the shrew's diet. To support this compulsive appetite, a shrew has to hustle. Its time is limited: the shrew has one or two families and dies of old age at perhaps 18 months. In that brief interlude shrews are constantly on the move, never holding still for examination by the casual observer.

Though shrews look remarkably like woodland mice, they are no relation. Shrews are members of the small order Insectivora, whose only other representative on the North American continent is the mole. In my experience—and to my initial surprise—the subterranean moles are easier to see than are the terrestrial shrews. One August day, I was working slowly through thick undergrowth down a bank of a stream called East Fork, a few miles southwest of Highlands, North Carolina. I had just come out onto a dirt car track when I saw a chunky mole about four inches long bustling across the track. I was wary of picking it up because moles, while not as vicious as shrews, are still biters.

To keep the mole from skittering off, I used my foot to block each escape route it chose until finally it sat still. It was shaking a little, either with fear or pent-up energy, but I could see from its tense little body that sitting still did not come naturally. Moles are on the go day and night, sometimes driving more than 100 yards of tunnel daily in the search for the grubs and insects they eat. Swimming through the ground with their enormously developed shoulder and foreleg muscles, they burn so much energy that in 12 hours without food they would starve.

The mole's abandoned tunnels are used as highways by anything small enough to fit through them, from snakes to rodents such as mice and voles. The latter two are probably the most abundant mammals of the forest floor. But, being largely nocturnal, they are seen less often than are chipmunks and squirrels. When I do hear what I imagine to be mice or voles scratching through the leaves by day, I rarely manage to catch a glimpse of them. On the few occasions when I have, it was because I disturbed a nest. Even then, the adult rodents made themselves scarce so fast that I could not tell what species they were. I know that voles have smaller eyes and ears than mice, with a generally stouter

SCARLET SNAKE

SCARLET KING SNAKE

CORAL SNAKE

The attractive but poisonous coral snake (bottom) has two harmless mimics, the scarlet and scarlet king snakes. Both differ from their lethal look-alike by their shorter length—16 inches instead of 28 inches—and the black band separating the adjacent red and yellow bands of the coral snake.

build and shorter limbs and tails. But the only people who really see much of these small animals are zoologists—after specimens have been captured in traps.

A far more visible forest animal is the skunk, which, because of its greater size, is easier to see—and occupies a higher place in the food chain. One night in early autumn I found myself alone in one of the shelters put up by the Park Service along the Appalachian Trail at a point called Mollies Ridge, where the trail runs through the Tennessee portion of Great Smoky Mountains National Park. Like all the shelters in the Smokies, it was a three-sided structure of stone, with the fourth side open to the air but protected by heavy Cyclone fencing. Before the open side was closed off, there had been trouble with black bears searching hikers' packs for food and breaking down the wire-bottomed bunks with their weight—which can be upwards of 500 pounds.

No bears came that night, but I was awakened by some sort of animal rummaging and clattering around only a few feet from me. When I flashed a light through the wire bunk bottoms, I saw a skunk. The situation called for restraint; precipitate or intemperate measures, such as chucking a boot at the animal, were plainly counterindicated. So I settled for keeping the flashlight beam steadily on the skunk, in the hope that it would conclude that its immediate surroundings had somehow become uncomfortable. Perhaps my theory worked, or perhaps the skunk just lost interest, but it wandered unhurriedly toward the door and out through a gap near the bottom of it.

Next morning, a few yards from the shelter, I found a hole alongside the trail maybe three inches deep and twice as wide. I figured the skunk had dug it, looking for something in the wide range of items it would consider edible: mice, snakes, eggs, berries, wild fruits, worms, insects, or one of the dozens of other items in its omnivore diet.

The three largest creatures of this forest, occupying the top end of the food chain, are primarily plant eaters. The deer is strictly herbivorous, while the black bear (pages 104-115) and wild boar usually elect to fill their cavernous bulks with enormous quantities of berries, nuts and small roots. Yet both bear and boar, strictly speaking, are omnivores, theoretically capable of eating anything up to and including rabbits and even deer—providing they could make the catch, which they rarely, if ever, even undertake.

A far more conscientious omnivore and, to me, the most intriguing of the lot is the little gray fox native to the Southern Appalachians. The adult gray fox weighs no more than 13 pounds and stands only a foot high at the withers, but has nonetheless been clocked running at 35 miles an hour. It can climb trees, shinning up vertical trunks if necessary. It has 42 teeth, which is 10 more than any fox hunter has, and in other respects, as well, may be the fox hunter's superior. The phrase "he out-fox-huntered me," for example, has not entered the language. For a long time I had held the quite mistaken impression that the animal's speed, agility and dental equipment aided it only in the pursuit of such prey as small rodents and birds.

One autumn day I came across a gray fox—or rather, a gray fox came across me—near a West Virginia highland plateau with the lyrical name Dolly Sods. The day was fresh and breezy, with little puffs of cloud riding high in the sky. I was somewhat nervous because it was bow-hunting season. But I figured the odds on my survival were longer than they would have been during gunning season, and I tried to lengthen them further by not moving around. While I was sitting quietly at the foot of a small beech tree I saw the fox. It came out of some shrubs and stood for a moment, testing its surroundings. I was downwind and motionless, so its warning systems—nose, ears and eyes—failed to pick me up. Satisfied there was no danger about, it trotted easily across the clearing at whose edge I sat, and then disappeared.

On the prowl for birds or mice or rabbits, I thought. The fox-in-the-hen-house idea. But I later read that scientists discovered the following items in the stomach of a fox killed one August in the Smokies: five dung beetles and traces of another; traces of a spider; 30 grasshoppers and 22 grasshopper eggs; one carrion beetle; and 12 pokeweed seeds. Another gray fox, killed in the Tennessee foothills of the Smokies, was discovered to have eaten 70 per cent invertebrates and 30 per cent vegetation. Another had eaten 95 per cent crickets, and the remainder other insects and centipedes. The stomachs of still other foxes have been found to contain maple seeds, persimmons, acorns and even, on occasion, the small mammals such as mice and chipmunks that I had assumed constituted most of a fox's diet.

To me, the fox's catholic eating habits seemed to be a near-perfect manifestation of the full-circle life plan of the forest floor. Directly or indirectly, every living thing in the forest is dependent on everything else for its existence and survival; each creature, no matter how small, has its own critical place in the order.

After the little gray fox was gone, I noticed one of the smaller creatures—a bumblebee, lumbering around from one blue aster to the next, making the flowers lurch and sway under its weight. The bumblebee was dusty with pollen, busy gathering stores against a winter it would never see: except for the next year's queens, all bumblebees die in the late summer or in the fall.

But the bee was commonplace compared to another insect that caught my eye among some blue-and-purple gentians near the asters. At first just its shiny blue-black head and thorax stuck out of the ground, looking like a huge science-fiction ant. When I rousted the insect out of its hole with a twig, I saw from its immense abdomen that it was an oil beetle—so named for the oily substance it exudes from various parts of its body to repel predators. Overall, it was about an inch long. The insect's head and legs seemed little more than an insignificant donkey engine, totally inadequate to drag around its bloated black sausage of an abdomen. On its back were two flimsy shields, covering wings that somehow manage to lift the beetle off the ground. Inside the hole from which I had urged the beetle was a mass of yellow eggs, which would hatch into larvae that parasitize bee's eggs.

Sometime from now—maybe weeks, maybe months—those larvae would launch into a kind of insect odyssey. The tiny larva first must find a plant frequented by bees, then climb up to the flowers and attempt to hitch a ride on a homeward-bound bee. It can complete its growth only by raiding the bee's eggs and food store. But the larva faces incredible odds: it must find the right plant, then the right insect, then it must survive in a nestful of hostile bees. The operation seemed to have about as much chance of success as my hitting a particular star in the Milky Way with a .22 on an overcast night. What strange liquors or perfumes, waves or rays, guide the larva on its blind search?

The thing was beyond my imagining, as were a million things about the swarming, teeming menagerie underfoot and all around. I thought of the boy I had been, turning over rocks in the Virginia Blue Ridge, tantalized by the network of tunnels below with their promise of whole unseen communities. If there had been a system of surface lights to mark the hiding places of the unseen animals, a system like the one I used to envision, the forest floor would have been a carpet of fire.

Shy Giants of the Hills

PHOTOGRAPHS BY SONIA BULLATY AND ANGELO LOMEO

Black bears have been a common part of the life and lore of wilderness travelers in the Southern Appalachians for at least 400 years. Yet even today popular concepts about these bears still contain a surprising percentage of fiction. Among common misconceptions are: bears are stupid; they have poor hearing and sight; they are fiercely aggressive; during hibernation they fall into an unbroken sleep for months on end; and they are indeed black.

To clear up some of the confusion and to get a more thorough understanding both of behavior and life cycles, scientists (including a psychologist) from the University of Tennessee began a study of the bear population of Great Smoky Mountains National Park in 1969. They also hoped to learn how the Park Service could continue to protect the bears from the millions of visitors, and vice versa.

The black bear—or *Ursus americanus*—that the scientists observed weighs about 250 pounds at maturity and while on all fours stands some three feet at the shoulder. And although nearly all members of the species in the Smokies and elsewhere in the East are black, in other parts of the country they turn up in various shades of brown, tan and cinnamon. Furthermore, though science has classified them as carnivores—largely on the basis of their tooth structure—their diet is 80 per cent vegetarian.

As to their hibernating habits, it turns out that though bears do go into what is known as winter sleep, their body temperature and metabolism remain near normal and they wake from time to time.

The impression that bears lack intelligence may derive from their somewhat awkward, lumbering gait —a result of the hindquarters being longer than the forelimbs—and an impassive facial expression. In fact, scientists speculate that they may be nearly as bright as primates. In the fall, for example, they have been observed climbing trees to eat acorns before they fall to the ground where deer might get them.

Regarding the keenness of its senses, the black bear's ears and nose are as sensitive as a dog's, its vision comparable to a monkey's. Finally, though they are thought to be ferocious, black bears are extremely shy. When confronted with any kind of threat they usually indulge in some mock heroics—and then scamper away, or climb a tree.

Scouting its terrain, an adult bear looks down from a fir tree. Amazingly agile for their size, black bears learn to climb trees as cubs and go on doing it all their lives—to look around, to retreat from danger, to rob a bees' nest of its honey or merely to take a nap. Propelled by their powerful hind legs, they shinny up, circling the tree in a spiral. They descend tail first, land on their rumps, roll over and amble off.

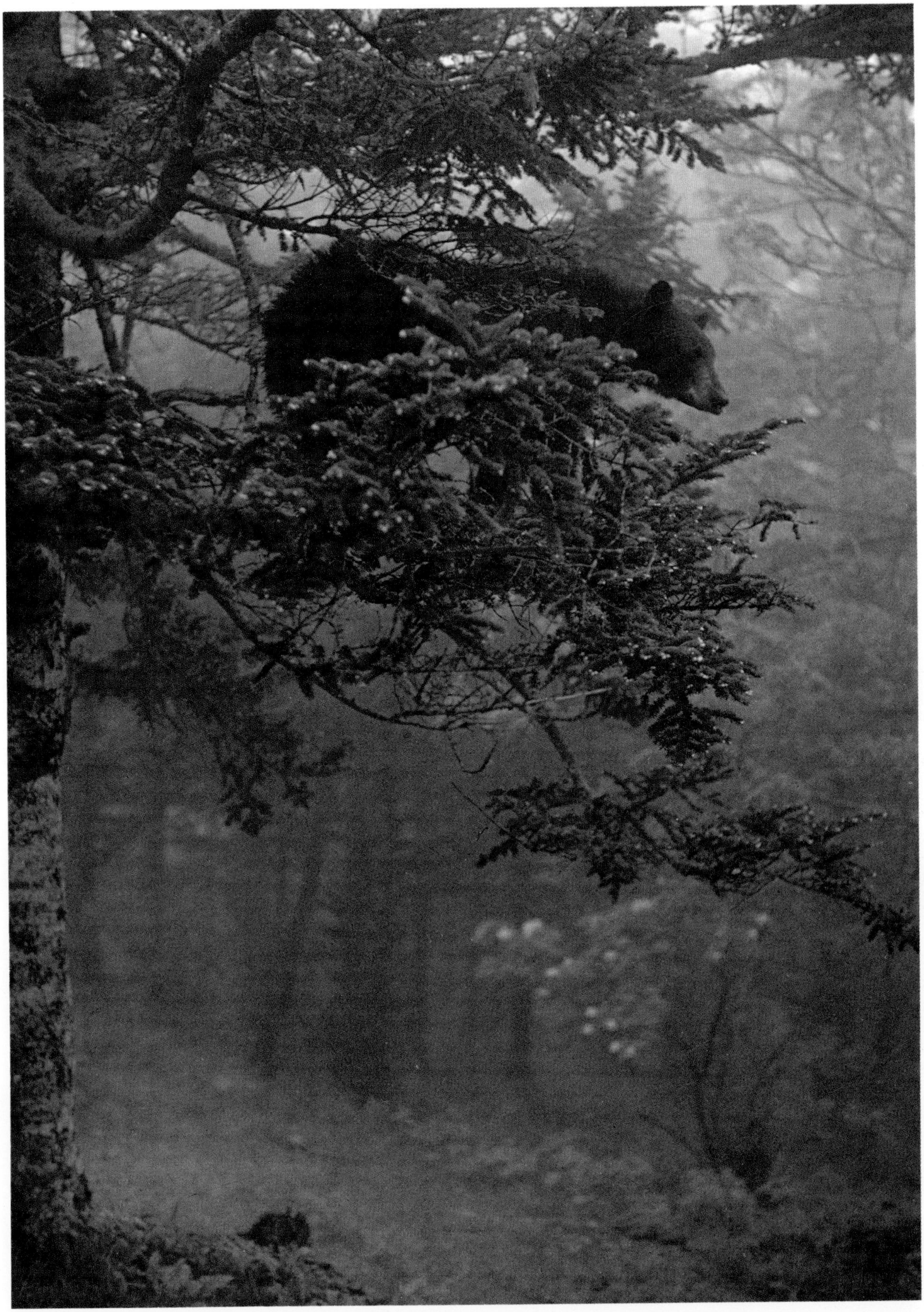

106/ Shy Giants of the Hills

The Games and Lessons of a Cub's First Year

In January or February, usually every other year, a female black bear —called a sow—gives birth to two or three cubs. Weighing only half a pound at birth, about the size of a rat, blind, toothless and nearly hairless, the cubs are born while their mother is half asleep in her winter den. Unable to do much more than suckle, they nurse quietly for the first few weeks, during which time their dozing mother may hardly be aware of their existence.

Some two months after birth, the cubs are ready to leave the den. They weigh about five pounds, are playful and active, and have full coats of fur —which may be a different shade for each cub. The mother is very watchful at this point, keeping the cubs from straying, and teaching them by example how to burrow for small animals, select the ripest berries, swim and climb trees.

The mother enforces her authority strictly, with hoarse grunts and hard cuffs of her paw. But she is indulgent, too, and the cubs have plenty of time to build their strength and coordination in games of tag, tumbling and wrestling, in which their mother sometimes joins.

A sow keeps a close watch on her two cubs, which are about six months old and weigh 15 pounds. They will have gained only another 25 pounds by the time they den up in the winter, reserving most of their growth for the next three years, and reaching their full adult weight at about four years old.

108/

Sensing danger, a sow stands guard while her cub scampers up a tree.

A cub scrounges for morsels among rocks and rich July foliage

Thoroughly relaxed on a precarious perch, a cub dozes in the sun.

Shy Giants of the Hills /109

nding easily upright on its hind legs, a six-month-old bear cub licks crushed insects from its paws while under the surveillance of its mother.

110/ Shy Giants of the Hills

Its ears cocked back, a black bear attempts to stare down the photographer, presumably hoping to frighten her off.

A Formidable Repertoire of Threats

Studies of black-bear behavior—especially relating to aggression and defense—are extremely difficult to conduct, for the animals prefer solitude and are shy of humans. But because some bears in the Smokies have become accustomed to panhandling on park roads, the University of Tennessee scientists have been able to observe them and extrapolate some conclusions about their backwoods brethren.

Apparently black bears' behavior is very much the same for both offensive and defensive situations. In either case a bear goes through the following sequence (which may include a number of variations):

First, when confronted with potential danger the bear will sniff the air and stare fixedly ahead. It then makes a mock attack, stopping anywhere from three to 20 feet away, and slaps one or both front feet on the ground or on a tree or bush.

Besides the slap, the bear emits a loud huffing noise. If that does not scare off an intruder, the bear rapidly snaps its jaws, at the same time popping its lips together. The animal may repeat these gestures, ending with another charge.

While Sonia Bullaty was taking the pictures on these pages, she found herself an anxious witness to these threats. She did not then know that black bears seldom carry a charge through to actual attack. Usually they veer sharply at the last instant and run away.

Having failed in its first threat, the bear slaps a rock with its paw and gives a loud huff.

Gnashing its teeth, the bear prepares to charge. Ten feet from the photographer it fled.

A Varied Diet for a Gourmand Appetite

Black bears' principal food—especially in the Appalachian woodlands—consists of such seasonal vegetation as huckleberries, beechnuts, fir and pine seeds, leaves and roots. However, they will eat just about anything, including pieces of tin cans and bits of glass. And although they eat little meat, given a chance they gorge themselves on fish, carrion and a variety of insects, most notably carpenter ants, grasshoppers and bees. They have been seen scratching open anthills, waiting until the insects swarm over their paws and then licking up the tiny morsels wholesale. Black bears will also rip open beehives and devour bees and honey indiscriminately, apparently unbothered by the stings.

Though armed with formidable teeth, bears are too lazy to be consistently successful hunters of large game such as deer. Sometimes, however, they are able to dig out mice, chipmunks, woodchucks and squirrels from their burrows. Moreover, a tiny bear cub that has wandered away from its mother may occasionally fall prey to attack from the adult male, which evidently does not recognize or respect a cub as young of its own species.

During the summer, bears tend to eat haphazardly, as the mood strikes them. But as fall approaches, they begin to stuff themselves on acorns and hickory nuts in order to build a sufficient layer of fat to nourish them through the winter.

An adult eats a meal of huckleberries, one of the black bear's favorite summer foods.

Shy Giants of the Hills /113

A female bear dines on white snakeroot leaves. A bear's menu in Appalachian forests may include over 50 different kinds of plants.

An adult bear prowls a hardwood forest during a misty midsummer dawn in Great Smoky Mountains National Park. Not hunted here—as they are in national forests of the Southern Appalachians—the black bears in the sanctuary seem to have stabilized their population at 400 to 600 animals.

Shy Giants of the Hills /115

4/ The Living Water

In the midst of so much wilderness, shivering flowers lean on the lip of torrents suddenly quiet, running over white quartz rocks and fragments of mica and garnet and gold in the dark sand. DONALD C. PEATTIE/ GREEN LAURELS

Eons ago, the Little River followed a meandering loop near the line that divides Blount and Sevier counties in eastern Tennessee. In the springtime, when the rain-swollen river swept down from its source on top of Clingmans Dome, some of the water would spill across the narrow neck of the oxbow, and instead of winding all the way around, would take a shortcut and rush directly downhill. Finally the river won its way; the water cut through the sandstone neck for good. Ever since then, the stream bed, rather than descending the mountain gradually around the length of the loop, has dropped abruptly at the point of the ancient breakthrough.

The result is a beautiful series of cascades shooting down water-worn sluices into basin-like potholes. Called the Sinks, these holes are carved here and there along the stream bed by the action of the swirling water. At the foot of the last chute, the clear, cold mountain water foams downward in a 20-foot-high cascade and collects in a pool about 40 feet across.

Small though the pool may be, it is big by the standards of the Southern Appalachians. In these mountains, which never bore the weight of glaciers, running water remains free for the most part to find its way downhill, unimpeded by ice-gouged lakes or barriers of rocky debris. Thus hardly any standing water occurs naturally in the higher mountains. Instead, there are thousands of little runs and torrents, joining together as they leave the hills to form larger rivers with an assortment of musical names: the Rappahannock, the Monongahela, the Big Sandy, the Peedee, the York and the James, the Potomac, the Cumberland, the Tennessee and the Little Kanawha. These streams and rivers, like the forests through which they flow, support the richest diversity of fauna in any like-sized region in North America. The waterways of New England are home to only 26 native species, and the Great Lakes-Saint Lawrence basin to only about 112; in the Southern Appalachians some 300 species have been identified.

Among the fish of the Southern Appalachians are some exceedingly showy creatures. The tangerine darter, endemic to the Tennessee River drainage system, displays an orange underbelly, crimson head and contrasting fins of orange and blue. In the same water system swims the iridescent blue spotfin chub, which requires a habitat of clean water and is thus threatened by the silt from dams constructed in the area during the past four decades. Exotic contours distinguish other Southern Appalachian fish, such as the hornyhead chub, which during the spring breeding season sprouts thornlike protuberances called tubercles on its pectoral fins and head. Only the males of the species have tubercles: they use them to hold the female securely during the spawning act and to fight other fish.

Ichthyologists studying the rivers of the Southern Appalachians have estimated that at least 50 species of fish are found only in this particular region of the country, but some varieties from foreign waters are by now as completely at home here as are the natives. Smallmouth bass, for example, not strictly indigenous to the area, apparently worked their way from warm waters to the west through a complex network of rivers. Other game fish such as the rainbow trout, a Western native, and brown trout, originally from Europe, were first brought into the streams of these mountains by state fish and game commissions and United States fisheries and wildlife agents during the late 19th Century. Today, all three of these once-alien species thrive here, much to the delight of anglers.

I decided that the best way to explore the life of these streams would be to dive right in among the fish and swim with them. I had gone skin diving in the Red Sea, the Mediterranean, the Caribbean, the South China Sea and the Strait of Malacca near Malaysia. I had explored the depths of fresh-water lakes, too, for hours on end. But I had never dived in the rushing waters of a clear mountain stream, and I had always wanted to give it a try.

On a trip to Tennessee, therefore, I asked in a Knoxville diving shop about the possibilities, and was put in touch with a skin diver named Rex Sentell, who was studying ichthyology at the University of Tennessee. The problem, Rex told me, was that the lower and slower reaches of rivers in the Southern Appalachians were likely to be so murky with mud churned up from the riverbeds that you couldn't see anything. And for the most part the higher reaches were likely to be too shallow for grown men to immerse themselves in. Rex had, however, dived in the Sinks. He said the pool at the bottom of the last little cascade was 10 to 15 feet deep, perfectly clear and full of fish. It would be an ideal spot for him to take underwater photographs of some of the species he was studying while I indulged my layman's curiosity about stream life.

The autumn sun was warm on the afternoon we picked to go to the Sinks, and we were hot by the time we had tugged our way into our wet suits, gloves, boots and helmets and had strapped on our scuba tanks. But the waters of the Little River run through the shade of deep woods for the most part and had lost little of their mountain chill even by the time they reached the Sinks, nearly a vertical mile below the summit of Clingmans Dome. When I slipped into the pool after Rex, the cold hit me like a sudden blow. It was a minute or so until the thin layer of water trapped between me and the rubber suit had warmed to a comfortable temperature. I had miscalculated how much weight I needed in my belt to overcome buoyancy, and I had to kick hard to propel myself down to the bottom after Rex. Once there, I had to hold on to an old sunken log in order to remain down. There were some sizable boulders and rocks strewn all around and so I piled some heavy stones in my lap until I was positive I would stay put. Finally I could settle back to look about.

I found myself sitting on the floor of a chamber 12 or 15 feet high, roofed in moving silver. Around me the watery world was olive colored, taking its hue from the algae that thinly coated the rocky floor, the almost-vertical walls and a jumble of dead, waterlogged tree trunks. I tilted back and looked directly up at the sun, whose rays were filtered by the water so that the sunlight appeared as nothing more than a bright patch in the general silver of the restless roof. Near the surface, where the turbulent water under the cascade was whipped full of air, little bright bits of light were captured in a thousand tiny spheres that winked out as each bubble floated back up to the surface, and winked

In the course of its trip down Clingmans Dome, Little River plunges into the lowest of a chain of pools known collectively as the Sinks.

back on again as new ones were churned back down into the water. Golden rays streamed through the glitter, illuminating the olive room.

It seemed very strange to me at first that I could see no sign at all of plant life other than algae. But then I realized that the physical problems caused by the current and scouring by ice, each tending to wash away the bottom where a plant would take root, make life difficult —even impossible—for larger aquatic plants. As a matter of fact, scientists still find it something of a mystery that such a sedentary form of life as algae succeeds in colonizing in the fast-moving headwaters of mountain streams. Nevertheless the algae manage to flourish even in this seemingly inhospitable environment.

Fish seemed to find the little pool in the Sinks every bit as congenial as did the algae. I saw dozens of rainbow trout just beneath the silver ceiling, facing directly into the swift current below the cascade. The trout held themselves in place with swimming motions almost too subtle to detect. Once in a while, an edible morsel would flow almost directly into a fish's waiting mouth.

Leaves came whirling and dancing along, but the trout paid no attention to these vivid yellow and red splotches of autumn amid the muted colors of their environment. All sorts of smaller flecks and specks drifted by, but most of these did not appear to interest the fish either. Occasionally a trout would dash from its position to snap something up and then, as often as not, spew it right out again.

As veteran fly fishermen know, a trout's sense of touch, taste or smell, or a combination of all three, is so acute that even the best imitation fools the fish only until the object gets into its mouth. This is the reason why trout are almost never hooked deeply by artificial dry flies, which are clever replicas of the aquatic insects that the trout feed on. Often, of course, they are not hooked at all, because a trout's vision is also so exceptionally keen that it will not be lured into going after many imitations.

The high quality of the trout's vision has led to much angling lore, of course, and also to a lot of conjecture from scientists as to just how good the fish's eyes really are. Trout do appear to have excellent color vision, which helps them in selecting food and also may be a factor in enabling them to distinguish between their own and similar-looking species during the breeding seasons, when trout, like many other fish, develop brighter markings. A number of scientists have concluded that, in addition to sharp color perception, trout have superb depth-of-field vision; that is, they can focus sharply on nearby and far-off objects simultaneously. This allows them to maintain their position in the stream by sighting on some fixed point on the bottom—a log or boulder for instance—while sifting out what is and what is not food from the stream litter drifting past them.

Deeper down than the rainbow trout, smallmouth bass had sorted themselves out according to their sizes. The smallest ones darted into the pool momentarily and then flashed back to the shallows; the medium-sized bass hovered well above the stream bed; and the biggest—weighing about three pounds—rested under the sandstone ledges at the bottom. On the way down to the spot where I now was sitting, I had perceived these big bass only dimly as moving shadows amid the darker shades of the ledges.

Frequently mixed in among these bass are brown trout, tough old-timers that are often larger and heavier than the bass and their fierce competitors for shelter and food. But they were nowhere in evidence as I surveyed the surroundings. In fact, for a moment, all activity seemed to be at a standstill. The pool's few big brown trout, a species not above bullying any of its neighbors, must all have been resting, uninterested in feeding even though plenty of minnows and crayfish were within easy reach just outside the ledges. The time of day—around noon—accounted for the temporary tranquillity of the pool.

Most fish in these streams usually feed in the early morning or late afternoon, apparently taking their cue from the angle at which the sun's rays strike the pool. Sometimes, too, they are triggered to feed by a rainstorm, which darkens the atmosphere, stirs up the water and flushes many aquatic insects out of their customary hiding places. Between feeding times the lion lies down with the lamb pretty regularly underwater. As I sat there, in the sun-brightened pool, a peace seemed to prevail that provided me with an excellent opportunity to observe how the trout and bass managed to maintain their truce boundaries.

The bass had more shelter from the current's force in their ledges down at the bottom of the pool. Up above, the trout had fewer natural buffers to help them, and they had to work a bit harder to maintain their places in the stream. A trout, however, would first be one place in the water and then, with a motion so fleet as to be hardly perceptible, it would reappear in another. The trout were fluid, part of the water's essence. In sharp contrast, the bass, slab-sided and tough, shouldered their way around the water, flexing their deep bodies with what appeared to be greater effort.

The difference is in some part explained by the configurations of the two species. Fish such as trout that inhabit fast-moving waters are usually torpedo shaped; fish that live in calmer waters tend to be more flattened, like bass or sunfish. The torpedo shape is far more streamlined, enabling trout to work the fast water efficiently; bass are much more comfortable in the quieter waters well beneath the stream's surface. Both kinds of fish, however, expend as little energy as possible to maintain their holding patterns. Each species searches out some kind of shelter or relatively quiet eddy in the pool. They face directly into the current not only to position themselves in the path of any food traveling downstream, but also to present the least body surface to the rushing water and to permit the maximum amount of the oxygen-bearing water to flood through their gills.

Swimming together in the pool at the foot of the cascade, the trout and bass were at the borderline of two different worlds—one in which they would mingle, the other in which the trout would reign supreme. For the relatively clumsy bass, the 20-foot-high cascade was an insurmountable barrier and chances are none of them would ever manage to go beyond it to the chilly headwaters upstream. Furthermore, it is doubtful that any of them would go even if they were able, since warmer, stiller pools are their preferred environment. The trout, on the other hand, could use their great speed to negotiate the cascade and feast on the bounty of insect life above it.

In the miniature world of the Sinks, it seemed to me that the bass and trout had sorted themselves out amicably. The situation was not without potential tension, however. Brown trout, being aggressive and canny, usually survive in these streams a lot longer than either rainbow or bass, reaching a length of 25 inches in about seven years. Over that span, a tough old brown trout develops a piscivorous appetite, learning to vary its usual fare of insects and crustaceans with small bass, rainbow trout and even a few tender young of its own kind—an abhorrence of cannibalism prevails only among some of the higher animals; brown trout abide by no such niceties.

I didn't actually see any squabbling among the fish in the Sinks, though. From my comfortable seat, I contented myself with watching how the fish seemed to slip into and out of sight. This disappearing act is, in fact, a means of protection from would-be predators such as fish-loving birds and mammals—and other fish.

Both the bass and the trout have a natural camouflage: their own

The meticulously detailed 19th Century engravings at right delineate three of the most popular and abundant game fish in Great Smoky Mountains National Park. Of the trio, only the brook trout is native to the area. The rainbow was transplanted from the West by federal fish culturists in 1880; the largemouth bass was brought in from lowland ponds even earlier.

The Living Water /123

RAINBOW TROUT

BROOK TROUT

LARGEMOUTH BLACK BASS

shading, which enables them to blend in subtly with their backgrounds. Most fish, in fact, share this disguise mechanism. From a bird's eye view, the fish's dark dorsal surfaces blend its bulk into the color of the deep water around and below it. Conversely, its pale belly, seen from below, renders it almost indistinguishable from the light at the surface of the water. This phenomenon is known among ichthyologists as obliterative shading.

Besides the camouflage of its basic coloring, a bass or a trout has the ability to resort to an actual change of color. Through a complex biochemical process, the hue of a fish's skin under its scales can adapt to match the color of its surroundings. Ichthyologists are still wondering just how this marvelous process might be triggered. In the course of puzzling, one awestruck scientist called it "the most wonderful automatic cryptic device in existence."

None of the fish in the pool where I had submerged seemed to be alarmed by the sudden presence of a monster from outer space. The bass down near my level went placidly about their business as if I weren't there at all, sometimes coming so close that I could see the golden-red irises of their eyes. To the trout above me, the bubbles from my breathing apparatus must have seemed no different from the thousands of other bubbles rising to the top of the pool. From top to bottom, the cascade produced considerable turmoil in the water. In all the turbulence it seemed that the water would be breathable, even to a human being, and that if I lost my scuba gear I could get along, just like a fish, on waterborne oxygen.

For a fish, of course, the oxygen supply in these waters was more than generous. Cold water can carry more oxygen in solution than warmer water, and white water under a falls or in a rapids tends to have a higher oxygen content than the water in a quiet pool. Both facts are important for trout, whose active lives in the fast waters they inhabit cause them to use oxygen at a much higher rate than do fish that inhabit still water.

But for me all that oxygen was inaccessible and, after perhaps three minutes at the bottom, I set off to explore the rest of the pool while there was still a good supply of air in my tank. I jettisoned the stones that held me down and began to swim slowly downstream, first looking in on the big bass underneath the ledges. I was hoping that they would stay put until my eyes got used to the darkness of their lair so I could see what they were up to back there deep in the shadows. But they were far more wary than the smaller bass that lived out in the open, and they fled from their shelters when I drew close to them. A crayfish —a fresh-water crustacean that looks like a lobster—was pottering around on the bottom, paying me no mind at all as it went resolutely about its business.

I headed toward the edge of the pool farthest from the cascade, out where the water was much shallower. I swam straight into a school of shiners, members of the minnow family not more than an inch or two long with silvery sides that flash in the sunlight. There are some 65 species of shiners in the Southern Appalachians, most of them indistinguishable to the layman. When I got up close I could see that the shiners around me had reddish snouts that made them look as if they were all suffering from bad colds. When I described them to Rex afterward he was able to identify them more accurately from my account. They were saffron shiners—a species found in many of the smaller waterways of the upper Tennessee River drainage system. The shiners had been given that name not for their red noses but for the yellowish fins of the males in breeding season.

The stream bed here in the shallows looked noticeably different from the bottom of the deeper part of the pool; instead of boulders and large rocks, the floor was strewn with gravel and pebbles. The colors of the shallow water, of the drifting leaves and the pebbled floor were considerably more intense than they had been in the olive-green depths of the pool. A long tree branch, thickly plastered with bright leaves on the side that faced upstream, lay across the stream bed, and I took up my station just above the branch.

This particular enclave of aquatic territory seemed to belong to a young rainbow trout, which was hovering a yard or so away from me on the downstream side of the log. To a diver water acts like a magnifying lens, causing things underwater to look larger than they really are; even so, making allowances for the optical distortion, I figured that the fish was no more than six inches long—about two years old. The little trout never darted more than a few inches in any direction after drifting debris, which seemed odd in the light of scientific reports I had read stating that the trout instinctively defends a quite sizable territory from interlopers.

It had been my understanding that a trout takes charge of an area several feet, or even several yards, in diameter; once the trout has established a claim, it does its best to chase all other members of its species away. The explanation for the trout's possessive behavior, some scientists believe, seems not to be what one might think—that the animal is guarding a food supply. Instead, in following its territorial impulse, the fish is probably defending a site for spawning and a shelter from the current. The size of the realm a fish regards as its own is to a great extent determined by the sizes of rocks and other obstacles that offer protection against intruders on the stream floor. Here near the lip of the pool, with natural refuges all around, the trout stood guard over a relatively small domain.

Besides the territorial instinct, there is another reason why trout—in fact, all fish—tend to restrict their movements as much as possible: they can literally die of fatigue. They can swim quickly in short bursts; brown trout, which are champion swimmers, have been clocked at 440 centimeters a second—that comes to about 10 miles per hour—but muscular exertion causes them to accumulate a chemical compound called lactic acid in their tissues. (Mammals build up lactic acid too, but at a much slower rate.) Too much of this substance can have a harmful effect on a fish's body. In normal circumstances, the animal instinctively combats potential danger by resting; a fish must rest six to 12 times longer after effort than does a mammal. And during these quiet periods, the acid works its way out of the fish's system. A fish denied the respite it needs tends to fare badly. Therefore, any sustained demand for energy, such as a sudden increase in the speed of a stream during a flood, takes a toll on the fish population.

The phenomenon of lactic acid build-up partially explains why hatchery trout, born and reared in relatively still water, do so poorly when introduced into streams where resident fish already claim title to the best available resting places. In territorial squabbles with newcomers, the better-conditioned native fish tend to emerge dominant. The hatchery fish, under continual harassment and bullying, have little chance. They drift helplessly downstream till they die of starvation, or they accumulate lethally high levels of lactic acid. Apparently, the weakened state of hatchery fish makes them easier for fishermen to fool with artificial flies. Their vulnerability is compounded by the fact that they have lived on free handouts and are accustomed to the great shadows of men suddenly looming above them. In streams where hatchery trout are regularly planted many of the fish are caught their first few days at large. Few survive a full season.

The shrewder native fish are much more wary and conserve their energy from the relentless current in part by seeking out stills and eddies —or by hunkering down in a chosen spot. Probably the most tenacious

A young stonefly, its four still-undeveloped wings indicating a recent emergence from the nymphal stage, perches on a dandelion in the Smokies. The mothlike insect, which is no more than an inch long as an adult, spends its early life in the water, completing its metamorphosis on the same submerged rocks and plants where the eggs were laid. Stonefly nymphs feed on plant life in the water and, in turn, serve as food for fresh-water fish such as trout and bass.

squatter in this particular pool was a little fish—a sculpin, I later found out—which I suddenly noticed only a few feet away from me. Not that it had materialized suddenly. It had been right there all along, but was so perfectly camouflaged by its coloration that I did not recognize it as a fish until it moved.

The sculpin was three or four inches long and its olive body was mottled with dark brown so that it was nearly invisible among the moving shadows of the shallow riffle. At first I thought the creature was some sort of small sucker, but it didn't have the outward-thrust lips of a sucker. It had the general body shape of a catfish but lacked the characteristic fleshy projections, called barbels, around the mouth. The sculpin was a brand-new fish to me, and I was obliged to go to Rex for help. I found him still moving around in the deeper pool, taking pictures of the rainbow trout. He followed me back to the sunken log and when we got there we discovered that the little fish had stayed in exactly the same spot. Rex and I stood up in the stream; he identified the fish and then told me to go back underneath the shallow water and take a careful look at how the sculpin maintained its position.

The sculpin's pectoral fins were large and rounded. The fish held them forward against the pebbly stream bed, with the fringes of the front pair in constant, rippling motion. The purpose of this stance was to deflect the current up over the fish's back, thereby pushing the creature down against the bottom of the pool. Meanwhile, the sculpin used its pelvic fins as a kind of brake system to help keep it from being swept away downstream.

Having explained the fish's modus operandi Rex went back to his picture taking, and I moved away from the well-lodged sculpin to look around the sunny riffle some more. The water was just deep enough to allow me to float, and I pulled myself along by scrabbling for hand holds in the stream bed. Pretty soon I came across a crayfish that was moving about by much the same method, although with considerably more grace and assurance. Like the fish, the little crustacean allowed me to come as close as I wanted. I knew from prior experience in crayfish hunting that had I been walking alongside the stream, sending tremors through the ground, the crayfish would have scooted away immediately. But apparently it was not programed to flee from floating underwater leviathans.

On the other hand I may have come across an eccentric crayfish. For one thing, it faced downstream; usually they head upstream, like almost all the other animals that live in moving water. Normally crayfish eat debris off the bottom but the mouth parts of this one were working as if it were grabbing infinitesimal bits of food out of the current. Its legs were in motion, but not in such a way as to propel its body. Instead it was moving them up and down, something like a person shifting weight from one foot to another.

Furthermore, the crayfish was not supposed to be abroad at all in the daylight; they usually forage during the night. Unfortunately, I only learned about the conventional behavior of crayfish some days later when I related my observations to an ichthyologist at the Smithsonian Institution. Apparently, a crayfish heading downstream and eating in the daytime is a real anomaly. Had I known that at the time, I would certainly have stuck around to find out what all these curious maneuvers were leading up to.

By sticking to the bottom the crayfish was using yet another common means employed by other river creatures in handling the problems caused by fast-moving water. Down by the floor of such streams is an aquatic stratum that scientists call the boundary layer, which moves relatively slowly due to the drag of the stream bed. In general, this zone ranges in depth from about a third of an inch to an inch and a quarter, growing narrower wherever the creek picks up speed. But this ribbon of water remains comparatively calm even in the fastest stream, creating yet another resting place and good feeding in the bargain. For if the layer did not exist, neither could most of the small invertebrates that spend their lives there and that in turn contribute an important source of nourishment for the fish.

As I crawled along the bottom in my crayfish posture, I began to notice how ingeniously the tiny invertebrates clung for dear life to that boundary layer. Thanks to a previous diving experience, I had no trouble imagining what it must be like to be a lightweight insect caught in a stream's buffeting current. Years ago, I was foolish enough to go diving in foul weather down to a shipwreck in 30 feet of water off the Atlantic coast. The currents on the bottom came in violent jerks and surges from one direction after another, up and down and sideways. The water was so wild and visibility so poor because of the churned-up sea floor that I could no more tell which way was up than if I had been tumbled by a comber rushing toward shore. I grabbed hold of a piece of the wreck, which served as my only point of reference. Having only hands instead of grappling hooks, however, I was quickly forced to let go.

Luckily I finally found the anchor line and followed it back up to the boat on the surface.

A few of these small stream creatures avoid being swept downstream by the means I had used to stay put in the deepest part of the Sinks: by loading ballast aboard. The larvae of caddis flies are prime examples of this technique. These wormlike creatures have salivary glands in their heads, which exude a kind of sticky silk. Using this substance as binder, they build cases from stream debris in which to live; other kinds of caddis-fly larvae manufacture these shelters from twigs or bits of leaves; still others use pebbles or grains of sand. I spotted a few of them moving slowly along the stream bed, hauling along cases that looked like miniature golf bags. The cases serve principally to protect the soft-bodied larvae within them, but marine biologists have noticed that mussels and snails that inhabit fast water tend to grow more massive shells than those living in calm water. Scientists are now investigating the possibility that caddis-fly larvae accomplish something similar: they seem to build heavier cases when they are in running water than they do when they are in still water.

Other dwellers on the stream's bottom seem to find the grappling hook the best device for holding on. Stonefly and Mayfly nymphs, among others, have well-developed claws that catch and hold on the rocks in the stream bed.

Instead of claws some fly larvae have suction cups or hydraulic suckers on the bottoms of their bodies to fasten them to their moorings. Still other aquatic bugs are equipped with anchor lines. Black-fly larvae, for instance, can live in very swift currents by tethering themselves to the bottom with silky lines extruded from large salivary glands. Certain Mayfly nymphs are even equipped with bristly pads that work like the sculpins' pectoral and pelvic fins.

The riffle beetle—a tiny gray or black insect scarcely a quarter of an inch long—has bristles, too, but these bristles serve another purpose altogether. They function as an ingenious kind of scuba (self-contained underwater breathing apparatus), so effective it never needs refilling with air. The bristles trap a flat bubble of air on the underside of the beetle, from which it obtains oxygen through its spiracles, or breathing holes. At the outset the bubble, like all air, consists of 21 per cent oxygen, 78 per cent nitrogen and the remaining one per cent a variety of other gases. The normal, stable balance of gases becomes disturbed as the beetle draws oxygen from the bubble. But in a complex process called diffusion, the lost oxygen is replenished from the surrounding

130/ The Living Water

Grotto Falls, one of a succession of 30- to 100-foot-high cascades along the Roaring Fork, tumbles over a rocky ledge as the creek continues its four-mile journey down the flanks of Mount Le Conte toward Gatlinburg.

water and equilibrium is thereupon restored. The process is so efficient that the riffle beetle can remain below the surface of well-aerated water comfortably for months at a time.

The riffle beetle is somewhat unusual among stream insects in that it spends so much of its life underwater. More commonly, stream insects pass only their nymph or larval stages in the water and then, when they metamorphose into adults, emerge into the open air. Black flies and midges do this, as do May flies, stone flies, caddis flies and dragonflies. But for some aquatic insects, their career out of the water is often brief, amounting to little more than a mating flight and, for the females, a search for a suitable spot, in or over the water, to lay eggs. May flies may live underwater as larvae for three years, then emerge on the surface with glistening wings but lacking a working mouth with which to take in nourishment. One day later it is usually dead—hence its scientific name, *Ephemeroptera*.

Except for the fish, the crayfish and the insects, the other inhabitants of the stream remained invisible to me; they live under the sand and pebbles of the bottom and many are nocturnal.

They are not all tiny, either. A giant salamander called the hellbender is found in many Southern Appalachian streams. The biggest one on record was taken in 1946 in the West Prong of the Little Pigeon River, about 14 miles from the Sinks; this one was more than 29 inches long. I had seen hellbenders (sometimes called water dogs) in aquariums, but never in the wild. They are bizarre creatures with huge, flat heads, flat bodies a little narrower than the heads, and short legs. Wrinkled folds of skin run down each side of the hellbender's body. The whole effect is of some specimen slightly distorted by having been preserved too long in alcohol.

I set out to look for a hellbender. I knew that they often spent the day hidden under rocks or logs, only coming forth at night to lumber along the stream bottom, snapping up crayfish, aquatic insects and even small fish. It seemed to me that a giant salamander was most likely to be found in deep water, and so I turned around and went back along the stream to the lowest part of the pool's floor. I began poking around into the shadows under the same rocky ledges where the big bass lived. They took leave of their shelters at my approach, and waited a little way off until I completed my inspection.

The proper way to get hold of a giant salamander, I felt pretty sure, was to plunge your hand right into the darkness and see if you grabbed something large, agile and slimy. My somewhat halfhearted way, however, was to peer into the shadows for a minute and then go on to the next ledge. To my disappointment, I found nothing more exotic than the bass. And a good thing too, as I later learned when an ichthyologist informed me that an irritated hellbender can grab your finger in its teeth and neatly peel off all the skin.

After my fortunately fruitless hellbender hunt, I went back to the deep pool under the cascade and once again weighted myself down with rocks, determined to sit still and watch the silvery bubbles and the patrolling fish until my air finally ran out. Utterly at ease and detached from the world above me, I thought of how full of life the stream was despite the scarcity of sizable flora growing in the water. But in fact, there is plenty of plant life here in the Sinks to form the basis of a food chain. While many aquatic animals demand a diet of living vegetable matter, others are well adapted to feeding on decaying plant life. The golden leaves dipping and whirling in the water around me, as well as the tiny flecks of this and that filling the water and dancing in the slanting bars of sunlight, all amounted to a continuous banquet moving past Little River's inhabitants.

My meditations lasted for five minutes, until finally I decided to let the stream take me. Since my air was due to run out soon anyway, I again jettisoned the rocks in my lap and buoyancy lifted me until the current caught me. Like the leaves, I moved downstream with no effort at all, carried dreamily along in the flow.

I fetched up abruptly on a pebble bar where the stream left the pool and entered shallow riffles. As I rose up on my knees, the weight of the world settled on me, the air tank and my own body no longer made light by the water. The sunlight was brilliant, no longer dimmed by passing through water. The surface of the pool was blue, not shimmering silver. It was a beautiful world, this one I lived in, but not a bit lovelier than the one I had just been visiting.

The Raw Beauty of a Wild River

PHOTOGRAPHS BY J. ALEX LANGLEY

Not far from the village of Cashiers, North Carolina, on the flank of Whitesides Mountain, a thin stream issues from the rock of the Blue Ridge. Almost immediately, confined within a deep trough and fed by a network of neighboring brooks, it turns into a rumbling torrent—the Chattooga River, a wild waterway that has earned both the awe and the protective admiration of all wilderness travelers who know it.

For 50 miles the Chattooga boils across rocky ledges, plunges down falls and foams through cliff-bound gaps. Occasionally it pauses in brief runs through woodland stills (right), but only for a momentary rest before surging off through another stretch of rapids. In one four-mile section, just above its terminus in Lake Tugaloo, Georgia, the Chattooga flows through a gorge in the form of no fewer than 48 major rapids, producing a roar that drowns out all other sound. This is the part of the river that inspired the adventure novel and the subsequent motion picture *Deliverance* by the Southern poet James Dickey.

In the course of its brief but roilsome journey the Chattooga drops more than 2,500 feet in elevation, or an average of about 50 feet in every mile. This dramatic descent, together with a constricted channel, gives the water its frightening momentum. By comparison, on its 277-mile passage through the Grand Canyon, the Colorado River—regarded by many wilderness canoeists and raft runners as the roughest stretch of navigable white water in the world—drops 2,200 feet, or an average of only eight feet to the mile.

Throughout most of its length the Chattooga serves as the state boundary between South Carolina and Georgia. But despite this civilized function in a region that has been settled for so long, the Chattooga has remained one of America's truly wild rivers. On both sides it is closely hemmed in by steep banks, sheer cliffs and heavily forested approaches, all of which serve to keep the river free of the meddlesome hand of man. This quality of wildness, combined with raw, primitive beauty, caused the Chattooga on May 10, 1974, to be selected for preservation under the Wild and Scenic Rivers Act, which Congress passed in 1968. It was the first stream in the entire Eastern part of the United States to be so designated—a triumph for the conservationists who had lobbied for its selection.

Flanked by tall conifers, the Chattooga chuckles over a rock shelf that spans the breadth of the river. Such placid stretches are rare on this river, whose series of booming waterfalls must be portaged by canoeists and whose rapids are hazardous for even skilled white-water runners.

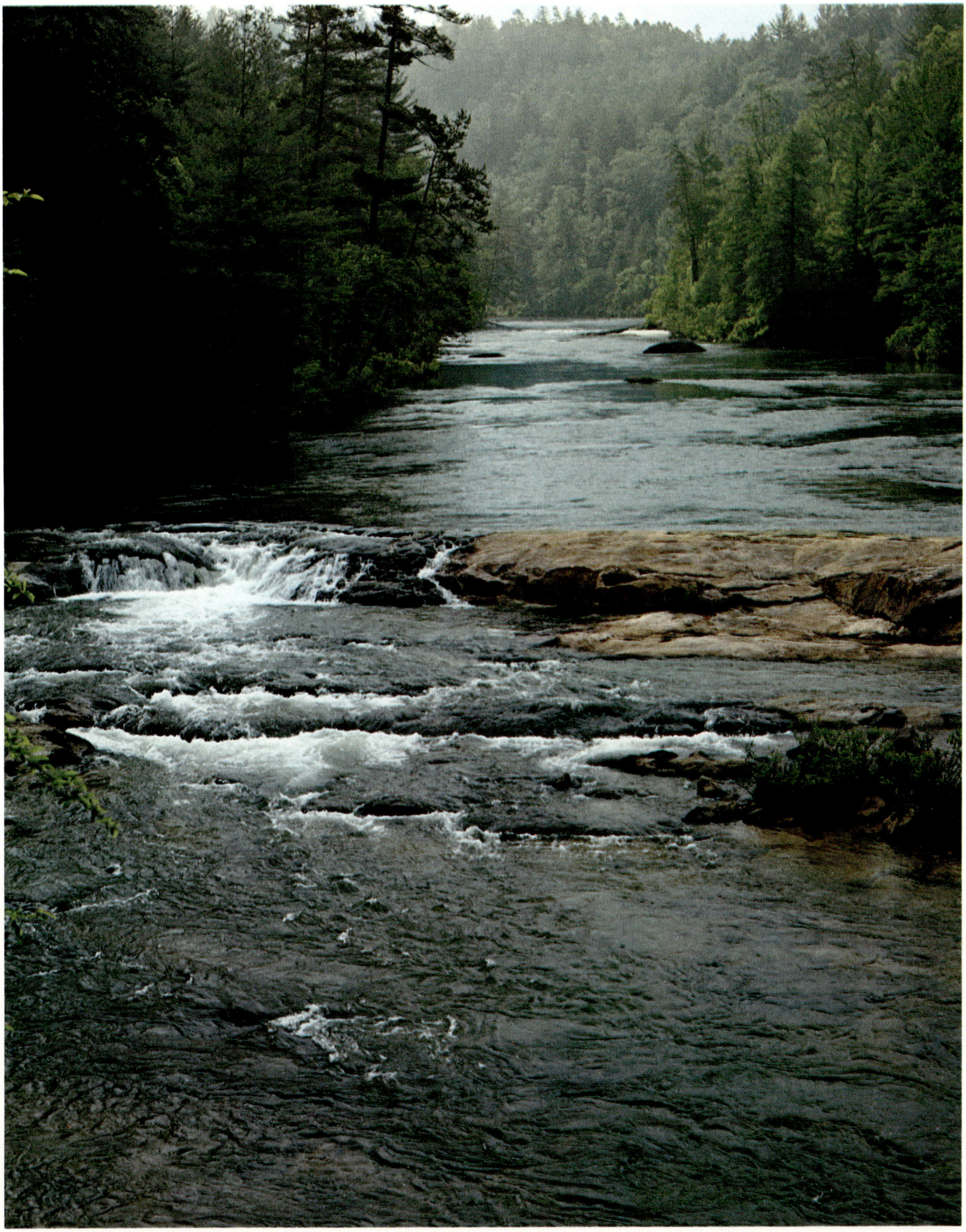

136/ The Raw Beauty of a Wild River

A tilted slab of gneiss rises 15 feet above the Chattooga's surface in a section of the river known as the Rock Garden. Once a thick, horizontal boulder, the rock had its right side eaten away by the river; the left side—through a fluke of the current—remained relatively unscathed so that its greater weight gradually tipped the rock to this startling angle.

A tributary leaping into the main river creates the 50-foot cascade of Dicks Creek Falls, considered the most beautiful cataract along the Chattooga.

Turbulent eddies mark the river's exit from an eight-foot-wide funnel called the Narrows, the most constricted stretch of the main part of the river.

The Raw Beauty of a Wild River /139

In its final three-and-a-half-mile run to Lake Tugaloo, the Chattooga rumbles over Woodall Shoals and fans out into treacherous water.

The Raw Beauty of a Wild River /141

Deceptively placid looking from upstream, Woodall Shoals claimed the lives of over a dozen canoeists in one recent 10-year period.

142/ **The Raw Beauty of a Wild River**

The striated gneiss face of Raven Rock Cliffs curves upward almost 200 feet to a lip jutting out over a backwater.

The pines and hemlocks of Georgia on the left and South Carolina on the right crowd the Chattooga's banks below Woodall Shoals.

In a climactic display of turbulence the Chattooga surges into a quarter-mile-long chute of white water known as Five Falls. Half a mile past the bend in the background, the river flows into the deep, still trough of Lake Tugaloo.

The Raw Beauty of a Wild River /145

5/ Echoes from the Ice Age

I passed into the deep forest,
And the dark night closed me round;
The dark spray flung its mist in my eyes,
The boughs crashed.

JOHN PEALE BISHOP/ LEAF-GREEN (A BALLAD OF THE BLUE RIDGE)

I must have been at the Boy Scout Manual age, perhaps 10 or 11, when I first read about the north woods. I wasn't clear on just where these north woods were, but I knew what they smelled like because I had a souvenir pillow from the state of Maine, stuffed with balsam needles. On it was written, "I Pine Fir Yew Deerly, and Balsam Too." The pillow made me dream of those distant, scary, sinister forests somewhere to the north.

In my mind they were dim, green-black woods where the wind moaned eerily and the fog snagged in tatters on the broken branches. They were the dark and terrible great north woods, stretching along under the roof of the world through Canada and Alaska and Siberia and Scandinavia, the woods of tarn and troll, loon and sasquatch, and the red-mouthed ghost of the wolverine.

Later in life, as I poked about in the mountains and valleys of the Southern Appalachians with fewer reveries and more facts in my head, I realized that I could, in effect, explore the great north woods right in the local terrain. As I gradually learned to see what was in the forest around me, I kept finding curiously misplaced elements of the subarctic, including conspicuous signs of the earth's recuperation from the ice age. And I discovered I could leap over a thousand miles or go back across millennia while walking around these Southern mountains.

To enter a coniferous forest like those of eastern Canada or New England, I had only to climb to the summit of North Carolina's Mount Mitchell. One day in the summer of 1974 I made such an expedition. The altitude on the mountaintop was over 6,000 feet, and though the month was August, the temperature was a chilly 65° F.—suggestive of the post-glacial climate in the region between Lake Huron and the Maine coast. The sky was the color of iron and sullen with the menace of storm. High winds drove fog streamers through the forest, making the fir trees creak. The trunks gleamed black with water, and when I walked over the thick, sodden moss that carpeted the forest floor, my steps made a squishing sound. Here and there between the snaking tree roots water stood in pools, still and dark as oil.

A cloud was enveloping the summit, and drops of condensation bellied under every twig and jiggled in the wind. But when the wind died for a moment, you could see that each drop was a lens that gathered the forest in and turned it upside down. Every tree, every crooked branch was there in reverse, a tiny miniature of incredible delicacy and precision. In the droplets—and in the real forest—I saw stands of red spruce and Fraser fir, which is a close cousin of the northern balsam whose heavy-scented needles had aroused my childhood daydreams.

Similar fragrant forests occur all across the heights of the Black Mountains: ancient woods, probably remnants of the coniferous forest that ranged over much of the North American continent as far back as 200 million years ago.

In the trees themselves could be read the harshness of the climate, which determined their ragged contours. I could see plainly that during the winter months, when the average temperature is 30° F., prevailing winds out of the northwest blew up the slopes of Mount Mitchell. Where a tree was exposed to the buffeting, its downhill side was bare of branches, all of them broken off by the weight of snow and ice plastered on them by the wind. But farther inside the forest, the trees had protected one another so that their branches were still arranged regularly on all sides of the trunks.

On the windward slopes of the mountain, however, even the hardiest of the trees were not particularly tall—few exceeded 40 feet —while on the leeward side they grew up to 70 feet. Nor were any of them very old; the wood of Fraser firs is weak, and a tree of this species usually succumbs to the elements within 50 years, before it has reached any great height. The spruces, though their wood structure is sturdier, tend to give way at about the same age. As further evidence of this vulnerability, I noticed there were blowdowns all around me. In a few relatively open places, several of the felled trees had gone down alone; since Fraser fir and red spruce are shallow rooted, the lone trees had been easy prey to the winds. In the thicker stands, however, these conifers had evolved a certain measure of support by intertwining their roots with those of their neighbors until the whole business was woven into a single mat above and beneath the surface of the soil. The trouble with the system was that when one tree went down, the others nearby tended to go as well. Thus, the forest here above the 6,000-foot mark had remained in a constant cycle of destruction and regeneration, as seedlings sprang up in the sunny openings created by blowdowns. It looked somehow impermanent; and yet it has looked this way for countless years, a true climax forest that probably will remain much the same for countless more years to come.

Spruce and fir tend to thrive in conditions like these all across the northern latitudes, relatively inhospitable regions of the world where the climate closely resembles that of the harsh period just after the last of the big glaciers receded. These places are, in general, too cold, too windy, too rocky or too shallow in soil for broadleaf trees to survive. An impregnable waxy coating, called cutin, makes the conifer needles almost weatherproof. The needles lose water vapor at a much slower rate than do broadleaves, so that the conifers can easily get through droughts in late summer and fall—in midwinter, too, when the temperature drops to zero and the ground freezes so solid that little if any moisture can pass through their root systems. The tiny conifer seedlings have an extra measure of drought protection: from the very start they have woody stems, whereas deciduous seedlings have moisture-demanding succulent stems and tend to wilt during dry periods.

I had planned to tramp all over the mountaintop, partly to see how far these tough veterans extended around Mount Mitchell's crown; and, too, I had wanted to see what else of interest I could find, here at the summit of the tallest peak in the whole chain. But the fog shrank the visible world to a radius of 50 yards or so. Sometimes the wind would pull the gray curtain apart for a moment and then close it in again, having briefly shown the tangle of wind-toppled trees or the black slanting spears of others not yet fallen but uprooted by storms and leaning crazily, dead, against their neighbors. Nevertheless, to see if I could get above the fog, I climbed the gray stone tower at the summit, erected in memory of scholar-explorer Elisha Mitchell for whom the mountain was named. But of course there was no view to be had there, either. Disappointed but hardly surprised, I came down from the tower to look around the woods some more.

Once conifers like these get established on their poor bits of territory, they defend their ground strongly. The acidity that the tannin in their fallen needles imparts to the soil not only discourages some insects that might attack the trees, but inhibits the growth of other plants as well. The lavish displays of wild flowers that burst out at lower altitudes in the Southern Appalachians are generally missing up here. Only the tiny blooms of wood sorrel, bluets, saxifrage, angelica and purple turtlehead appear on the heights in the shadow of the evergreens. The acid soil, together with constant shade and extreme weather conditions, almost eliminates the understory of shrubs found in the hardwood forests at lower altitudes.

The relative absence of a shrub layer made it fairly easy for me to walk through the Mount Mitchell woods—but it also cut down on the variety of habitats available to animals. "A dense continuous conifer forest is almost a biological desert," the naturalist Rutherford Platt wrote in *The Great American Forest*. Though scientists feel he overstated the case, it is obvious that while conifers take care of themselves, they don't leave much for the benefit of other living things.

However, there was at least one life form on Mount Mitchell that was not only uninhibited by the conifers but positively thrived in their presence. These were lichens, primitive plants that cling like barnacles to trunks, branches and twigs of spruces and firs—both living and dead—mottling the wood gray green or sometimes gray blue. They even nestled among the fir needles. Brittle, gray antler lichen interwove in loose bunches the size of my hand. Old-man's-beard, a mosslike lichen, hung from branches shaggy with other lichens, and writhing stalks of goblet lichen held out shallow cups fringed with prongs. The whole forest was festooned and made ghostly by the strange, pale growths.

Lichens are among the simplest and toughest forms of life on earth. Compared with them, the rugged conifers are frail, helpless things. They were the first bits of plant life to flourish on the barren rock exposed by the retreating glaciers. Some species grow at 18,000 feet on the frigid, stony slopes of the Himalayas, and others can thrive in the scorched aridity of the desert. Lichenologists—botanists who specialize in the study of these remarkable plants—have discovered that some specimens can survive deep frozen, at temperatures near absolute zero; others live through severe drought and high temperatures for several years.

There seems to be only one environment to which almost no lichen is suited: the big modern city. Few urban American parks still have the lichen growths they once had. Their progressive disappearance began to be noticed about a century ago, and scientists feel that one cause is the noxious gases from cars and factories that pollute city air. In fact, lichens are such efficient indicators of dirty air that, in some urban areas, they are used to monitor pollution.

In the clean air atop these mountains, however, the lichens flourish in their curiously symbiotic fashion. All lichens are a combination of algae and fungi. Certain species of each exist separately all through nature, but none looks anything remotely like a lichen. Scientists who have broken down lichens in laboratories found that the fungi from them just formed shapeless clumps, something akin to bread mold, by themselves. And these specific fungi are never found living free in nature, because they are not capable of producing fruiting bodies: they can be grown only in cultures. The algae from lichens, however, can exist separately like any other algae—as microscopic one-celled plants. When the two are put together, the fungi act as a supporting structure that obtains nutrients from the air and water; and the algae carry out the photosynthesis that manufactures food. The sum becomes an almost brand-new organism.

This organism, resulting from such a highly practical marriage, has a growth rate that is barely perceptible and an all but immeasurable life span. Some of the 25,000 species of lichen grow so slowly that the relatively short-lived scientists—here today and dead tomorrow—detect little change in size within their lifetimes. As for age, some lichen colonies have been estimated to be more than 2,000 years old.

Lichens undoubtedly grew on the top of Mount Mitchell before the spruce-fir forest took root. During the ice age, when there was a true timberline on Southern Appalachian peaks so that each high mountain had a bare, treeless patch on top, lichens must have proliferated on those seemingly barren patches. In fact, these curious plants played an active part in creating the soil that eventually made the mountaintops hospitable for the conifers. Lichens produce an acid that breaks down rock, gouging out tiny crevices and depressions. From these minuscule ruts, which give the lichens good footholds, crumbs of rock fall free and settle in cracks, making it possible eventually for the wind-blown spores of mosses to move in and take hold. The mosses grow and die and decompose, and catch airborne dust. Gradually over many thou-

Echoes from the Ice Age /151

A stand of striped falsehellebore graces the sedge-covered bank of a quiet stream in the Monongahela National Forest.

sands of years, as these processes continue simultaneously, soil forms —soil in which higher plants can find a footing. It must have taken tens of thousands of years for the rocky dome of Mount Mitchell to be transformed into full-fledged forest land. But from the time the process was at last complete—about 10,000 years ago—until now, the appearance of these woods has changed little.

While the cooler, high-altitude woods have changed little since the final glacial periods, the make-up of the relatively sparse animal population that inhabits them has undergone some drastic alterations. Toward the end of the ice age several of today's large fauna were already present —deer, caribou and bear. But they mingled with creatures that looked like characters in a nightmare.

The remains of these fantastic beasts turn up most often in limestone caves like those in West Virginia and eastern Tennessee. Once those caverns must have been home to them, and their fossilized bones are one of the rewards of cave exploration. Not being attracted to the sport of spelunking myself—the humidity, the chill and the hazards of falling over unseen precipices into black spring-fed pools do not appeal to me—I nonetheless share the spelunkers' prizes by reading reports and listening to tales of their finds.

Some of the earliest cave explorers to retrieve fossils hereabouts were miners. In 1810, men digging for nitrate to use for gunpowder came upon a huge claw, still bearing skin tissue, from the foot of a ground sloth. The rest of the creature's bones were subsequently recovered and reassembled to form a skeleton that now stands (in an Ohio State University museum) over seven feet high. From the shape of the bones, paleontologists reconstructed what it must have looked like in life—a long-furred, jowly creature that lumbered around on long-nailed feet, waving a big bushy tail. The ground sloth had rhino-sized cousins that grew to 20 feet in length and hauled around 10,000 pounds of flesh, blood and bones. Scientists have dubbed this ground sloth *Megalonyx jeffersonii,* after the nation's third President, who was fascinated by virtually all aspects of America's natural life, including its vanished giants. In 1801, Thomas Jefferson carried *Megalonyx* bones, which he had originally thought to be those of a giant lion, in his luggage when he traveled to Washington to take office.

In the ice-age world *Megalonyx* had plenty of extraordinary mammalian companions. From another Tennessee cave have come the remains of *Smilodon,* the saber-toothed tiger whose canine teeth measured eight inches in length. And in another, explorers have found remains of a mastodon, a beast comparable in size to an elephant, and once the most common mammal in Eastern North America.

But those ice-age species are gone now, having perished in a mass death that occurred around 11,000 years ago. The responsible agent, some scientists believe, was *Homo sapiens,* the hunter; many others claim it was climatic change—a rapid increase in temperature. It was probably a combination of both. In any case, most of the ice-age giants were gone, both from here and from most other forests around the world, by the time of the first recorded history. But they lingered on in one place—Madagascar (now the Malagasy Republic), off the southeast coast of Africa—where man apparently did not show up until near the end of the first millennium A.D. Giant lemurs, oversized hippos and huge flightless creatures called elephant birds were still present on the island in historical times. But they were quickly depleted until, finally, all were gone. It took man less than 1,000 years to wipe out the last of those ancient creatures.

My own unscientific notion is that we are still engaged in mopping-up operations, and that the Southern Appalachians are one of the battlegrounds. I suspect that before the white man arrived the Indians did the bulk of the work on the really big species. We like to think of the Indian as living in perfect harmony with nature, with a beautiful, almost mystical state of mutual respect existing between man and beast. But the fact is that 12,000 years ago, according to carbon dating of various fossils and artifacts, the Indian was here and the giant ground sloth was here, and now only one of them is left—though greatly reduced in numbers. The same is true of the saber-toothed tiger, the musk ox, the Pleistocene moose, the mastodon, the mammoth and all the other big animals that once ranged through the Southern mountains. I suspect the ancestors of the Indians only stopped wiping out species when they ran out of large animals that were slow enough to catch without too much difficulty.

Recent computer simulations suggest that the arrival of no more than 100 humans on the North American continent from Eurasia about 12,000 years ago conceivably could have led to the extinction of some 93 million giant animals in less than three centuries. The computers calculated that an original band of 100 people, supported by game as abundant as that which now inhabits the richest African game parks, could have multiplied to 300,000 in 293 years—a population sufficient to have wiped out the large animals completely.

A few fairly sizable though less exotic animals still remained when European man arrived on the scene around 1700. They were, notably, the elk and the Eastern bison, but they didn't last long against the guns of the whites. By 1800 these creatures were all but extinct in the Southern mountains. In 1825 the last known bison in West Virginia was killed at Valley Head in Randolph County. Since then, so far as anyone knows, the species has been totally extinct. The majestic elk hung on in the Southern Appalachians for a little longer. As late as 1873 elk were reported in West Virginia, near the headwaters of the Cheat River. That was close to the end, though, and any elk seen in the East since then have been reintroduced from Western herds.

A few other large animals remain, but the war against them started long ago—and still goes on. In 1716 His Majesty's Lieutenant Governor of Virginia, Sir Alexander Spotswood, led an expedition to the Blue Ridge Mountains during which members of the party sometimes killed as many as three bears in a day. Others have pressed the attack since that time with considerable, if not total, success. Bears still survive, however, particularly in the protected environment of the Great Smoky Mountains National Park, where the acorns and other food they eat are usually in plentiful supply.

Deer not only survive but thrive, despite the attempts of such great hunters as one James Todd of Rockingham County, Virginia, who gained a certain renown in the 19th Century by killing 2,700 deer with a single muzzle-loading rifle. Fortunately, deer are very resilient. While some Southern woodsmen were busy shooting deer, others were cutting over the forest. The felling of the climax trees opened the woods to dense lower growth, which provided hiding places and plenty of green twigs and new bark for the deer to feed on. As a result, the white-tailed deer appears to be even more common today than when the hunting began.

But the big ice-age predators are gone—and so, too, are the timber wolves that roamed all over the Southern Appalachians when the settlers first arrived. The last-known wolves in the Commonwealth of Virginia were killed on Clinch Mountain in Tazewell County during the winter of 1909-1910. Gone, too, is the small lion variously known as the cougar, the painter, the panther or puma, the mountain lion or the catamount. Or is it?

Except for a handful holding out in the swamps of Florida, the cougar has been presumed extinct all throughout the East for many years.

Fanciful formations like those at right, contoured over the centuries by the constant interaction of minerals and water, transform the limestone caves of the Southern Appalachians into an underground world of bizarre beauty. Disc-shaped shields extend from the walls of Grand Caverns, Virginia; more delicate anthodite "flowers" adorn Virginia's Skyline Caverns; and gypsum and selenite etch fragile patterns in Cumberland Caverns, Tennessee.

Echoes from the Ice Age /155

BRIDAL VEIL SHIELD

ANTHODITE FLOWERS

GYPSUM FLOWERS

DECORATED SHIELD

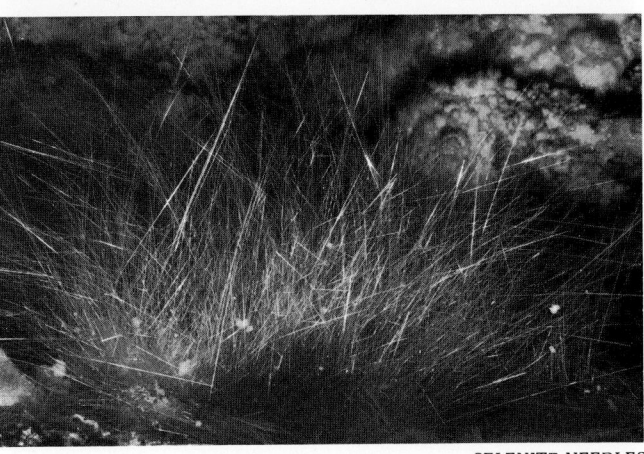

SELENITE NEEDLES

The gleaming surface of subterranean Dream Lake in Luray Caverns, Virginia —the largest cave in the East—mirrors the intricate shapes of stalactites, stalagmites and crystal shelves. Caves such as this one have been a rich source of relics—both of ice-age animals and of the Indians who later prowled the Southern Appalachians.

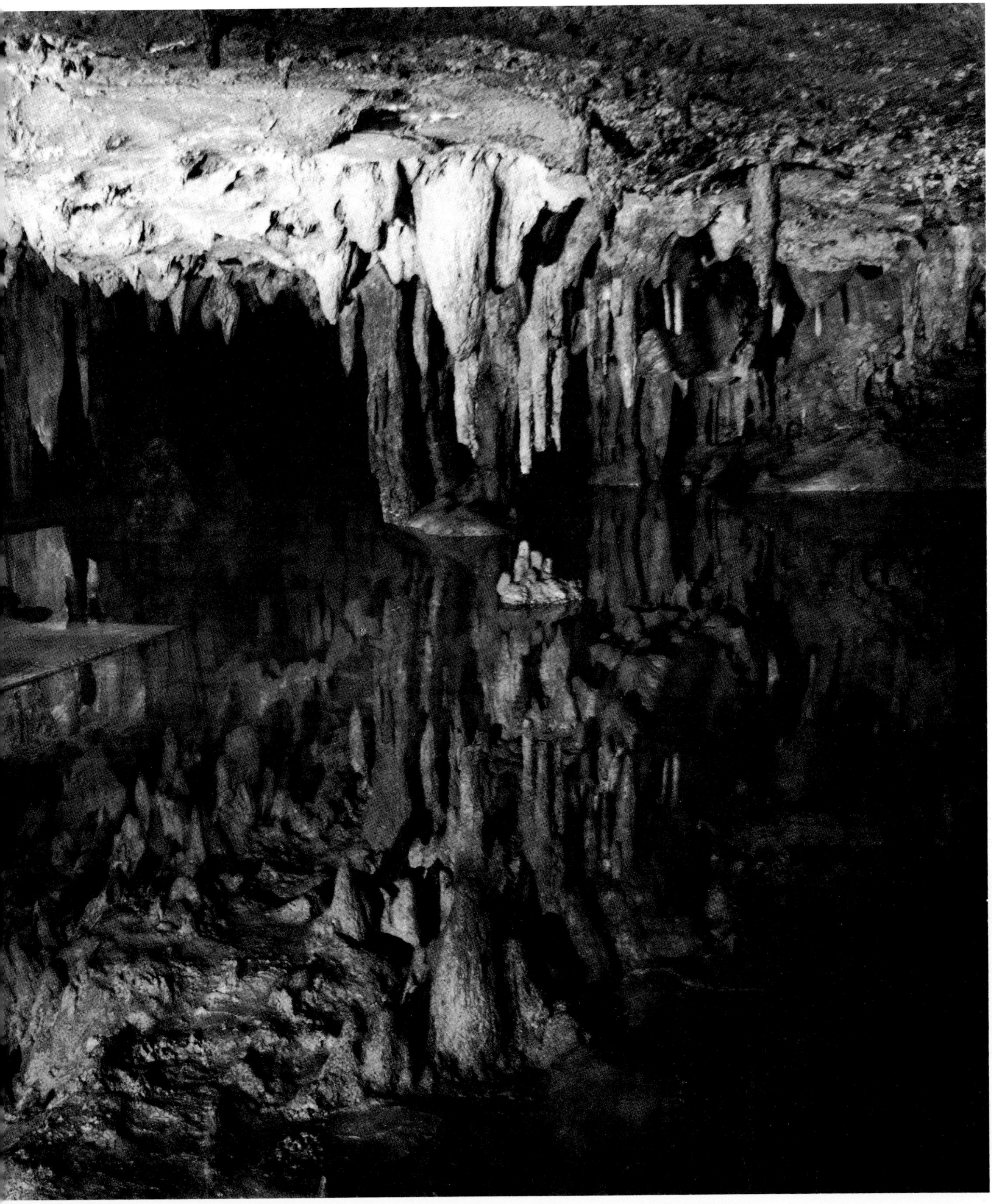

At least nobody has seen a dead one; and hunting dogs have treed no cougars. (The fact that these cats are notoriously easy to tree is one major reason why they got wiped out in the first place.) Plainly, then, the cougar has been extirpated in the Southern Appalachians.

And yet the reports keep coming in, very difficult ones to discredit. In 1962 a party of forestry students claimed to have seen a cougar at close range in the Monongahela National Forest in West Virginia. All members of the party were sure the animal was a cougar, and it is hard to see how they all could have been wrong. A cougar is big and has a long tail; a bobcat—another cat of the Southern Appalachians— is small and has a short tail. A dog can be the size of a cougar and have a long tail, but any six-year-old child knows the difference between a dog and a cat.

At close range there is just no way to mistake a cougar for any other animal native to the United States. Not if you know anything at all about wild animals, as did those forestry students. As did the college biology student who saw a cougar 25 yards away in 1973, in Virginia's Shenandoah National Park. As did the two Virginia game wardens who saw one 100 yards off in Rockingham County in 1973. As did the conservation officer who spotted one in West Virginia in 1972.

I prefer to think that all these people saw just what they thought they saw and that the cougar still lingers on in the Southern Appalachians as a sort of not-really-missing link between the saber-toothed tiger of the ice age and the household pussycat of today.

Though the well-explored caves of the Southern Appalachians have provided most of the area's trove of prehistoric animal remnants, some have been found in the numerous other natural storage lockers, the bogs, where a curious chemistry is continuously at work. The bogs of the Southern Appalachians are another physiographic phenomenon that commonly occurs much farther to the north. For example, bogs are common in Scandinavia, where peat cutters as well as knowledgeable scientific investigators often dig up vestiges of past life—deer, ax handles, a wooden wagon, even a few human corpses 2,000 or more years old, preserved throughout the ages by the high acid content of the moisture in the bogs.

The Southern Appalachian bogs, like those elsewhere, are lakes or ponds in the natural process of becoming dry land. In the Northern United States and Canada these small land forms-in-transition are known by the Algonquian Indian word *muskeg*, meaning trembling earth.

There, the lake basins were scooped out by glaciers. In the Southern Appalachians they are just geological irregularities that trapped water.

These bogs, where they occur in the Southern Appalachians, serve as the southernmost home for many plant and animal species common in more northerly country: American larch, black spruce, dwarf dogwood, bog rosemary, cranberry and buck bean. In addition, they contain weird carnivorous plants—the horned bladderwort, the sundew and the pitcher plant—that lure and trap insects, and then digest them. Snowshoe rabbits, which turn white in winter like weasels, inhabit these bogs, along with the Nashville and mourning warblers, Swainson's and hermit thrushes, purple finches and northern water thrushes. None of these birds breeds any farther south than the bogs of West Virginia. Moreover, the fir trees that grow in West Virginia's boggy Canaan Valley are misplaced populations of *Abies balsamea,* the species that provided the aromatic needles for my state-of-Maine souvenir pillow.

Most bogs in the Southern Appalachians exist at elevations of about 3,000 to 4,500 feet. But altitude alone does not explain why they support northern plants and animals. Canaan Valley lies at only 3,200 feet, and yet frosts have been recorded there every month of the year. The reason is that bogs create their own wintery climate. Even a miniature one can do so—as I found out one summer when I visited what must be one of the smallest bogs in the world. It was a hot day in late August when I set out to find the bog. I knew from the scientist who had told me about the place that it was near Shady Valley in eastern Tennessee, past a certain general store and down a certain road. And yet I walked by the bog twice before I spotted it.

The bog was not much more than five good paces across, no bigger than a smallish room in a house. It looked like a little clearing of brown grass, but as I stepped out onto it my feet began to sink in, and I drew back to take off my shoes and socks. I still was not sure I had found the right spot, but once I got back out onto it barefoot, I knew. I sank ankle deep into the mossy covering blanket of sphagnum and into water as chilly as a mountain trout stream. I had to bend over and look hard before I found what I was looking for—cranberries, still pale but just starting to be tinged with red, hidden down in the matted foliage of the surface. The air was blazing hot up where I breathed. But down where the cranberries lived, it was cool and damp. I could feel the chill just by holding my hand over the low-growing plants. Even this tiny bog had created its own miniclimate, making a hospitable environment for other northern plants like red chokeberry and swamp milkweed.

Spence Field, among the largest grass balds in the Southern Appalachians, covers some 40 acres in a carpet of bald oat and autumn bent.

The refrigerating fluid came from an underground spring that fed the bog; the insulation was sphagnum—a moss that grows on the water's surface, starting at a pond's edges and working its way toward the center. I pulled up a few strands of the stuff. Although the sphagnum was growing on the water, it looked pale and dried out in the late August heat. Like any other moss, it contains chlorophyll, but the green cells are surrounded by large, colorless, hollow cells. Below water these hollow cells fill up with water. Above the surface, however, they contain only air. By forming a dense carpet over the water, the moss effectively holds in the chill of the subterranean water. As some of the water evaporates through the sphagnum into the warm air, the air itself cools. The chilly air then settles over the depression in which the bog has formed.

I was intrigued by the little bog, but not satisfied. I wanted to study the whole phenomenon on a larger scale, and so at the crack of dawn one late fall day I visited Cranberry Glades, just west of Mill Point, West Virginia. The glades—the local term for bogs—cover 600 acres of bog land at an altitude of some 3,300 feet in the Monongahela National Forest. The bog itself stretched level as a lake in front of me for hundreds of yards, reddish brown in the light of the just-rising sun. Though I was at just about the same latitude as that of the old Southern town of Charlottesville, Virginia, I could have been, for all appearances, in northern Minnesota.

In spite of the cold, I went out barefoot onto the surface of the *muskeg*. The reason for the Indian name was immediately apparent: the terrain under me quaked and shimmied like a trampoline. It was clear that I was not standing on solid ground at all but on a tough mat of vegetation —sphagnum and pigeon-wheat moss—spread across the top of a partially backed-up stream. As I walked my feet sank down six inches or so, the clear, cold water welling up around my ankles. In actual fact, I was standing on top of water way over my head. The natural carpet under me was secure, but tales of wanderers lost in the bogs, unfortunates in both fiction and fact who vanished forever in gloomy bogs, darted across my mind.

What aroused my curiosity most at Cranberry Glades was the carpet itself, the mosses that, perhaps more than any other single factor, give the bog its special character. Both sphagnum and pigeon-wheat grow on top of a dead layer of their own species, producing new growth on top of old and thus forming a mat of steadily increasing thickness. Both

Near the summit of Clingmans Dome, a sunset haze veils imposing stands of red spruce and Fraser fir. Although both of these evergreens thrive at high elevations, only the fir can flourish at altitudes over 6,000 feet.

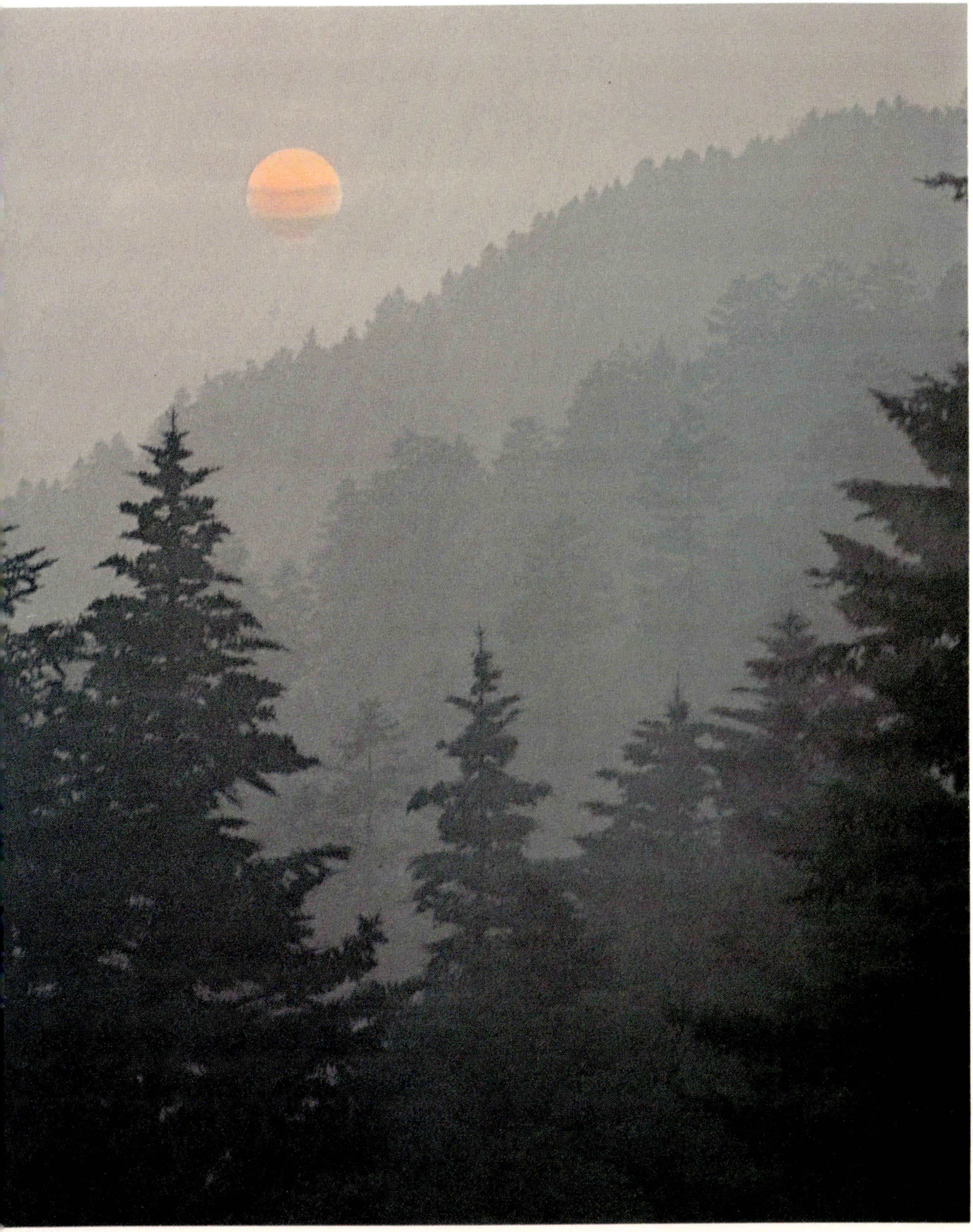

mosses, especially the sphagnum, generate in the water a strong solution of tannic acid—the same chemical used to preserve leather in tanneries. In consequence, the rate of organic decomposition is extremely low in bog water; and thus the bogs tend to preserve in death whatever creatures happen to drop into them. Over the course of years, new growths of moss on the surface push older growth down under, where instead of rotting away, it forms peat, a dense, fibrous organic mat. In Scandinavia, Ireland and elsewhere, peat farmers cut and dry bricks of this material to use as cheap fuel.

There was no chance that day of my sinking haplessly into the bog. Under the sphagnum, compacted layers of peat lay on top of algae-saturated ooze. And below that, I had read, was marl, clay laced with coarse sand filtered down through the upper layers—which measured about 12 feet altogether. Below that lay a 20-foot-thick build-up of clay, and under that, bedrock.

The process by which these layers had been made began with microscopic plants, animals and airborne dust floating on top of the lake or pond water. Over the centuries the plants and animals, as they died, sank to the bottom of the pond. In time, the accumulations raised the level of the pond bottom and built up a layer of sediment until one day the water was shallow enough so that larger plants could take hold, and sphagnum appeared on the shores. Bits of dead plants—limbs and leaves from the lake's now-blurry edge—and moss then added their weight to the matter beneath. The accumulated burden compressed the bottom of the muck into clay.

Eventually what you have in places like these is a soggy, waterlogged sandwich. The muck and mosses move toward the center at the rate of perhaps one foot every 15 years. The sediment and the peat become more and more dense, leaving less and less room for water, until finally the area becomes solid enough for the forest to take over. When that happens, the Cranberry Glades and other bogs will disappear—and with them will go the cold-climate plants and animals. The Southern Appalachians will have lost another one of their fascinatingly incongruous reminders of that other wilderness far to the north.

Yet changes like these are natural. And though I mourn the passage of any plant or creature or land form, however small, ultimately I can only marvel at the whole process of natural change. What I resent are the unnatural changes—of which man seems to be the principal agent. There is coal in the Appalachian hills, upon which industry has turned its covetous eye. If people go after the coal—and they well may—they will create strip mines, cutting huge troughs in mountainsides. When they have extracted the coal, barren swaths will remain in their wake, great sweeps of onetime forest, shaved clear of all visible plant life. The putrid air that has already driven lichens out of the cities may then invade the slopes, where it will kill the soft greens and blues that enrich every surface they grow on.

On a less lethal scale, but still intrusive, is the careless woodland visitor who, in his hunger to savor the freshness of the remaining wilderness, scatters his garbage over the forest floor. Litter will not kill the woods; they are too tough. But a forest paved with film boxes and drink cans is not, to me, a wilderness.

When I go back into these woods next time, I would rather not have to rely on my memory alone to bring me their freshness. I want to find the Southern Appalachians as they were when I last wandered into them. Two or ten or twenty years from now, I will want to revisit those small corners of difference tucked away in the vast sweep of one of the world's finest deciduous forests, where the seemingly insignificant anomalies stick in my mind, as the sight of an island stays with you long after the endless miles of surrounding ocean have been forgotten. I will want to savor the dun color of a grass bald in autumn, the towering trunks of tulip trees, the impenetrable tangle of rhododendron hells, the fog-wrapped, storm-torn mountaintop conifers, the silvery ceiling of my underwater haunt in Little River and the blush on the cranberries in my tiny bog near Shady Valley. And, always, the gentle, endless rising and falling of the mist-blue mountains themselves.

Winter Moods in the Smokies

PHOTOGRAPHS BY JOHN CHANG McCURDY

Winter settles uncertainly upon the Great Smokies in a moody tug-of-war between warmth and cold, rain and snow, sun and mist that lasts throughout the season. The first sign of winter may appear as early as September, when thin dustings of frost touch the fir-clad peaks. Meanwhile in the sheltered coves and valleys, plants are still flowering and bearing ripe fruit. But by October, when photographer John Chang McCurdy first visited the Smokies to record his impressions of the oncoming season, temperatures were dropping to 30°, and in the moist woods the morning hoarfrost was so heavy that, on at least one occasion (right), it appeared that snow had fallen overnight. By this time, the leaves were bright with new colors, while the summer hues of rhododendron and azalea petals, and the bright red berries of spicebush had vanished as blossoms shriveled and fruit dropped off the shrubs.

The weather proved to be capricious. Usually little rain falls in the autumn months; streams sometimes dwindle to mere trickles and choke with leaves (page 168), and the familiar bluish haze of the Smoky Mountains thins noticeably owing to the decrease in water vapor that during other seasons combines with the hydrocarbon exhausts sent up by actively growing vegetation. But McCurdy unexpectedly found himself drenched with rain from clouds that gave a brooding caste to the Chimney Tops as he photographed them through a brief break in the weather (page 178).

When he returned in February, hibernating animals were beginning to waken, buds to open, and one afternoon a brief shower of warm rain created a rainbow for him just before sunset. He appeared to have missed the chill of deepest winter, when as much as 38 inches of snow has been recorded in one month (at Newfound Gap), and the mercury has been known to drop below zero for five days in a row. But in another unpredictable turn of mood, the clouds suddenly dumped 15 inches of snow on the Smoky Mountains as McCurdy was photographing the season's final assault on the forest and the high ridges around Clingmans Dome (page 174). Almost as soon as it fell, however, the snow began to melt. As he walked through the whitened woods McCurdy could feel the ground soft beneath his boots. After five months, winter had finally given up the tug-of-war.

HEAVY HOARFROST ON THE FLANK OF MOUNT LE CONTE

DRY OCTOBER AT ROARING FORK FALLS

Winter Moods in the Smokies /169

A BLAZE OF YELLOW BIRCH AT SWEET RIDGE

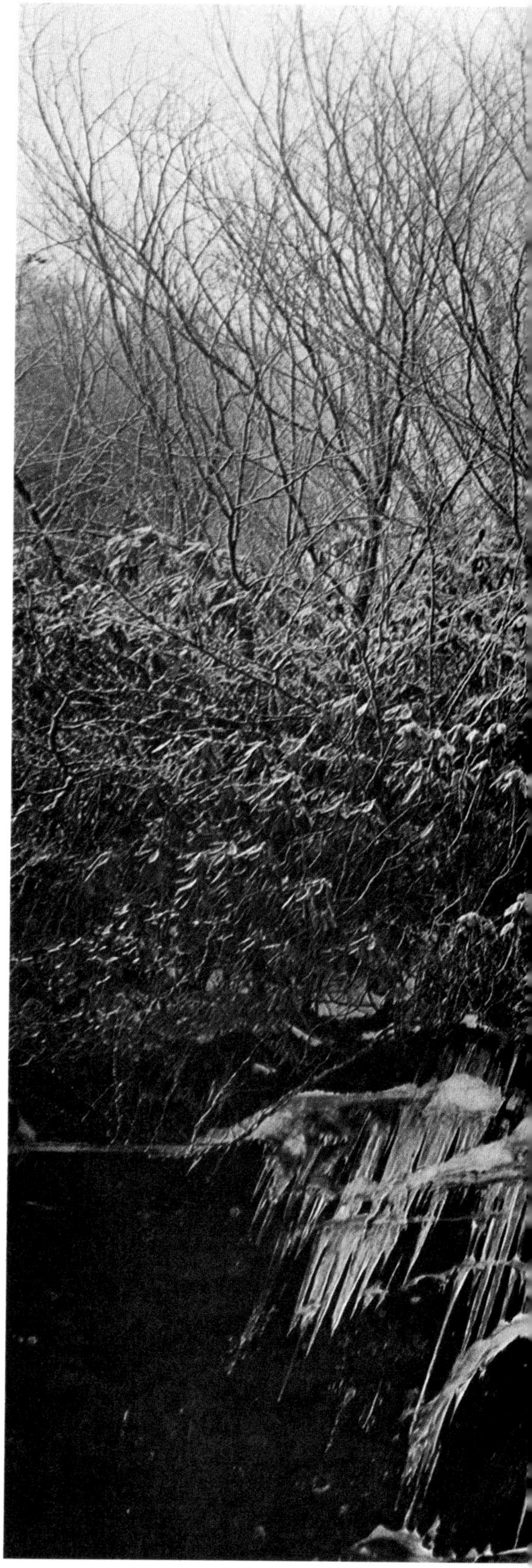

Winter Moods in the Smokies /171

A FROZEN COPSE OF RHODODENDRONS AFTER A MID-FEBRUARY SNOWSTORM

SNOW-CARPETED ROCKS ON A BANK OF THE LITTLE PIGEON RIVER

Winter Moods in the Smokies /173

A LACEWORK OF ALLSPICE BESIDE A CASCADE

174/ Winter Moods in the Smokies

THE APPALACHIAN CREST NEAR CLINGMANS DOME

/175

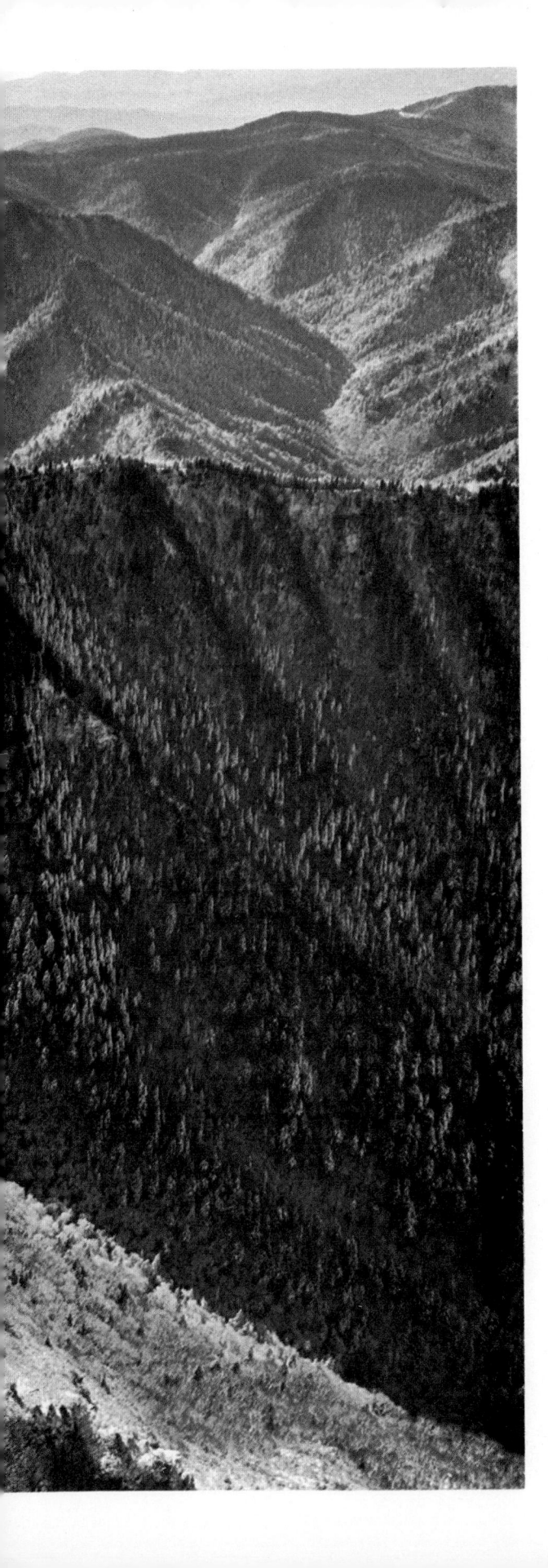

SNOW-DUSTED BEECHES IN THE NEWFOUND GAP AREA

RAINBOW'S ARC AT FIGHTING CREEK

178/ Winter Moods in the Smokies

THE CHIMNEY TOPS ILLUMINATED BY A CLOUD BREAK

/179

Bibliography

*Also available in paperback.
†Only available in paperback.

*Andrews, William A., et al., Guide to the Study of Soil Ecology. Prentice-Hall, 1973.

Brooks, Maurice, The Appalachians. Houghton Mifflin Company, 1965.

Brooks, Maurice, The Life of the Mountains. McGraw-Hill Book Company, 1968.

Cahalane, Victor H., Mammals of North America. The Macmillan Company, 1947.

Call, Richard Ellsworth, The Life and Writings of Rafinesque. John P. Morton and Company, Printers to the Filson Club, 1895.

Cochran, Doris M., and Coleman J. Goin, The New Field Book of Reptiles and Amphibians. G. P. Putnam's Sons, 1970.

*Coker, Robert E., Streams Lakes Ponds. The University of North Carolina Press, 1954.

Conant, Roger, Peterson Field Guide to Reptiles and Amphibians. Houghton Mifflin Company, 1958.

Cronquist, Arthur, Introductory Botany. Harper and Row, 1961.

*Dickey, James, Deliverance. Houghton Mifflin Company, 1970.

Drimmer, Frederick, The Animal Kingdom. Greystone Press, 1954.

Dunbar, Carl O., and Karl M. Waage, Historical Geology. John Wiley and Sons, 1960.

*Evans, Howard E., Life on a Little Known Planet. E. P. Dutton and Company, 1968.

*Farb, Peter, Living Earth. Harper and Row, 1959.

Federal Writers' Project, North Carolina, A Guide to the Old North State. The University of North Carolina Press, 1939.

Fenton, Carroll Lane and Mildred Adams, The Fossil Book. Doubleday & Company, 1958.

Graham, Alan, Floristics and Paleofloristics of Asia and Eastern North America. Elsevier Publishing Company, 1972.

Gray, Asa, Gray's Manual of Botany, 8th ed. American Book Company, 1950.

Harlow, William M., Inside Wood. The American Forestry Association, 1970.

*Harrar, Elwood S. and J. George, Guide to Southern Trees. Dover Publications, 1948.

†Holt, Perry C., ed., The Distributional History of the Biota of the Southern Appalachians. Part II: Flora and Part III: Vertebrates. Virginia Polytechnic Institute and State University, 1971.

†Huheey, James E., and Arthur Stupka, Amphibians and Reptiles of Great Smoky Mountains National Park. University of Tennessee Press, 1967.

Hynes, H. B. N., The Ecology of Running Waters. University of Toronto Press, 1972.

Klots, Alexander and Elsie, Insects of North America. Doubleday & Company, 1971.

Lagler, Karl F., John E. Bardach and Robert R. Miller, Ichthyology. John Wiley and Sons, 1962.

Linsenmaier, Walter, Insects of the World. McGraw-Hill Book Company, 1972.

McClane, A. J., McClane's Standard Fishing Encyclopedia. Holt, Rinehart and Winston, 1965.

Peattie, Donald Culross, A Natural History of Trees. Houghton Mifflin Company, 1950.

Peattie, Roderick, The Great Smokies and the Blue Ridge. Vanguard Press, 1943.

*Platt, Rutherford, The Great American Forest. Prentice-Hall, 1965.

Polunin, Nicholas, Introduction to Plant Geography. McGraw-Hill Book Company, 1960.

Ramsbottom, John, Mushrooms and Toadstools. Collins, 1959.

†Sharp, Aaron J., Carlos C. Campbell and William F. Hutson, Great Smoky Wildflowers. University of Tennessee Press, 1972.

Silvics of Forest Trees of the United States. U.S. Department of Agriculture, Forest Service, 1965.

†Stupka, Arthur, Trees, Shrubs and Woody Vines of Great Smoky Mountains National Park. University of Tennessee Press, 1964.

Stupka, Arthur, and Eastern National Park and Monument Association, Wildflowers in Color. Harper and Row, 1965.

Swan, Lester A., and Charles S. Papp, Common Insects of North America. Harper and Row, 1972.

Thwaites, Reuben Gold, Travels West of the Alleghenies. Arthur H. Clark Company, 1904.

Unsinger, Robert L., The Life of Rivers and Streams. McGraw-Hill Book Company, 1967.

†Van Doren, Mark, Travels of William Bartram. Dover Publications, 1955.

Periodicals and Bulletins

Berkland, James O., and Loren A. Raymond, "Pleistocene Glaciation in the Blue Ridge Province, Southern Appalachian Mountains, North Carolina." Science, August 1973.

Chilcoat, Terry S., and Michael R. Pelton, "A Black Bear Primer." Unpublished paper.

McKeon, John B., John T. Hack, Wayne L. Newell, James O. Berkland and Loren A. Raymond, "North Carolina Glacier: Evidence Disputed." Science, April 1974.

Whitehead, Donald R., "Late Wisconsin Vegetational Changes in Unglaciated Eastern North America." Quaternary Research, 1973.

Whittaker, R. H., "Vegetation of the Great Smoky Mountains." Ecological Monographs, Vol. 26, No. 1, January 1956.

Acknowledgments

The author and editors of this book are particularly indebted to Aaron J. Sharp, Distinguished Service Professor Emeritus, Department of Botany, and A. Murray Evans, Director of the Herbarium, University of Tennessee, Knoxville; Sidney S. Horenstein, Department of Invertebrate Paleontology, The American Museum of Natural History, New York City; Robert E. Jenkins, Assistant Professor of Biology, Roanoke College, Salem, Virginia; Alan Kelly, Fishery Management Biologist, United States Fish and Wildlife Service, Great Smoky Mountains National Park, Gatlinburg, Tennessee; Rex Sentell, Department of Zoology, University of Tennessee, Knoxville; Ralph M. Sinclair, Aquatic Biologist, United States Environmental Protection Agency, Cincinnati, Ohio. They also wish to thank the following individuals and institutions. In Georgia: Bob Harper, United States Forest Service, Gainesville. In Maryland: Richard Highton, Professor of Zoology, University of Maryland, College Park. In New York City: John Behler, Assistant Curator of Herpetology, and James G. Doherty, Assistant Curator of Mammalogy, New York Zoological Park; Clark T. Rogerson, Senior Curator, Cryptogamic Botany, New York Botanical Garden. In North Carolina: Lino Della-Bianca, Silviculturist, United States Forest Service, Asheville; Jack Kennedy, District Ranger, Pisgah National Forest, Marion. In Tennessee: Susan Power Bratton, Tremont Research Station, Townsend; Gordon Burghardt, Department of Psychology, Michael Pelton, Department of Forestry, and Ronald Peterson, Department of Botany, University of Tennessee, Knoxville; Glen Cardwell, Supervisor Park Technician, Don De Foe, Public Relations, and Edward Trout, Park Historian, Great Smoky Mountains National Park, Gatlinburg; Donley M. Hill, Limnologist, and Ben D. Jaco, Fisheries Projects Manager, Tennessee Valley Authority, Norris; Arthur Stupka, Gatlinburg; Zenith O. Whaley, Pittman Center. In Virginia: William E. Davies and John T. Hack, United States Geological Survey, Reston; Perry C. Holt, Professor of Zoology, Virginia Polytechnic Institute and State University, Blacksburg. In West Virginia: Kenneth L. Carvell, Professor of Forest Ecology, West Virginia University, Morgantown.

Picture Credits

Sources for the pictures in this book are shown below. Credits for pictures from left to right are separated by semicolons; from top to bottom by dashes.

Cover–Robert Walch. End papers 1, 2 –Sonja Bullaty and Angelo Lomeo. End paper 3, page 1–Peter B. Kaplan. 2, 3–Bill Gulley from Photo Researchers, Inc. 4, 5–Robert Walch. 6, 7 –Charles R. Belinky from Photo Researchers, Inc. 8, 9–Frank J. Miller from Photo Researchers, Inc. 10, 11 –John Dominis from Time-Life Picture Agency. 12, 13–Sonja Bullaty and Angelo Lomeo. 18, 19–Maps supplied by Hunting Surveys Limited. 23–John Dominis from Time-Life Picture Agency. 28, 29–Jim Amos from Photo Researchers, Inc. 32, 33–Frank J. Miller from Photo Researchers, Inc. 35–John R. MacGregor from Educational Images © 1975; Russ Kinne from Photo Researchers, Inc.–Mike Hopiak; Noble Proctor from Photo Researchers, Inc. 39 through 53–Sonja Bullaty and Angelo Lomeo. 56, 57–By permission of The British Library Board. 58–Forest History Society, Inc. 60, 61–United States Forest Service. 66, 67, 69–Sonja Bullaty and Angelo Lomeo. 72 through 85 –Robert Walch. 88, 89, 93–Jerome Doolittle. 94–Left Jerome Doolittle; right Rolland R. Swain–Alexander Limont. 95–Jerome Doolittle except right center Alexander Limont. 96–E. R. Degginger. 100–Z. Leszczynski from Animals Animals except bottom Patricia Caulfield from Animals Animals. 105 through 115–Sonja Bullaty and Angelo Lomeo. 118, 119–Jerome Doolittle. 122, 123–Culver Pictures. 126 –© Buddy Mays 1972 from Photo Researchers, Inc. 130, 131–John Chidester. 135 through 145–J. Alex Langely. 151–Robert Walch. 155, 156, 157 –Dan J. McCoy. 160–Jerome Doolittle. 162, 163–Sonja Bullaty and Angelo Lomeo. 167 through 179–John Chang McCurdy.

Index

Numerals in italics indicate a photograph or drawing of the subject mentioned.

A

Actinomycetes, food-chain role of, 92, 96, 97
Algae, 118, 120, 150
Allegheny Mountains, *cover*, 16, 22
Alum Cave Bluffs, 31
Alum Cave Bluffs Trail, 27
Alum Cave Creek, 30
Angelica, 149
Animals: in bogs, 159; extinction of, 153-154, 158; in food chains, 90-103; ice-age, 152-153, 158; introduced species, 26. *See also specific types*
Appalachian Mountains, 21-22. *See also* Allegheny Mountains; Blue Ridge Mountains; Great Smoky Mountains; Southern Appalachians
Appalachian Trail, 62, 101
Audubon, John James, quoted, 60
Azalea(s), 31, 38, 51; alpine, 84; flame (*Rhododendron calendulaceum*), *50-51*

B

Bacteria, food-chain role of, 92, 97
Balds: grass, *160*, 165; heath, or laurel slicks, 22, 31, 72, 84
Balsam, northern, 147, 159
Bartram, John, 56
Bartram, William, 54-55, 59, 66, 71; quoted, 54; *Travels*, 59; watercolor by, *56*
Bass, 122; color changing in, 124; largemouth black (*Micropterus salmoides*), *123*; smallmouth, 117, 121
Basswoods, 30, 38, 66
Bear(s), 65-66, 154; aggressive and defensive behavior, *110-111*; black (*Ursus americanus*), 101, *104-115*; cub rearing, *106-109*; diet, 104, *112-113*
Beech(es), 55, *176*
Bees, 102-103
Beetles, 97; oil, 103; riffle, 129-130
Birch(es), yellow, 30, 31, 62, 63, 73
Birds, 68, 159; native and migratory, 26. *See also specific types*
Bishop, John Peale, quoted, 146
Black Mountains, 23, *32-33*, 147
Bleeding heart (*Dicentra eximia*), 44
Blue Ridge Mountains, 21, 22, 26, *28-29*, 57, 72, 154. *See also* Black Mountains; Great Smoky Mountains; Linville Gorge
Blue Ridge Parkway, *18-19*, 24, 26
Bluets (*Houstonia serpyllifolia*), 80, *81*, 149
Boar, European wild, 26, 101
Bog(s), *4-5*, *158-159*, 161, 164
Brooks, Maurice, quoted, 36
Brown Mountain, 83, 84
Buckeye(s), 66; yellow, 30, 64
Bullaty, Sonia, 111
Buttercup (*Ranunculus acris*), 41, 43
Butterfly weed (*Asclepias tuberosa*), 42

C

Canaan Valley (West Virginia), 159
Cascade(s), *173*
Caves, 152-153; mineral formations, *155*, *156-157*
Chattooga River, *134-145*; Dicks Creek Falls, *138*; Five Falls, *144-145*; Lake Tugaloo, 134, 140, 144; the Narrows, *138-139*; Raven Rock Cliffs, *142*; Rock Garden, *136-137*; Woodall Shoals, *140-141*, 143
Cheat River (West Virginia), 23, 154
Cheat River Canyon, *10-11*
Cherry, fire, 37, 62
Chestnut(s) (*Castanea dentata*), 55, *58*, 64; blight, 63-64
Chimney Tops, 166, *178-179*
Clinch Mountain (Virginia), 154
Clingmans Dome, 24, 26, *88-89*, 116, 118, 162, 166, 174
Coleridge, Samuel Taylor, 86; quoted, 72
Columbine (*Aquilegia canadensis*), 38, 41, 42
Conifers. *See* Forests
Conservation: of black bears, 114; in Chattooga River, 134; endangered birds, 26
Coreopsis, 42
Cougar(s), 154, 158
Coves, as vegetation community, 22, 27, 38, 73
Cranberry Glades (West Virginia), 161, 164
Crayfish, 125, 127-128

D

De Soto, Hernando, 21
Deer, 25-26; white-tailed, *23*, 154
Dickey, James, 134
Doolittle, Jerome, 16

F

Fairy wand (*Chamaelirium luteum*), 41
Falsehellebore, striped (*Veratrim viridae*), 151
Ferns, wood (*Dryopteris spinulosa*), *66-67*; intermediate (*Dryopteris intermedia*), 83
Fir, Fraser (*Abies fraseri*), 26, 36, 60, 147-148, *162-163*
Fire pink(s) (*Silene virginica*), 44-45
Fish: endemic species, 117; hornyhead chubs, 117; lactic acid build-up, 126; obliterative shading, 124; saffron shiners, 125; sculpins, 127; shapes, 121-122; species variety, 117; spotfin chubs, 117; tangerine darter, 117. *See also* Bass; Trout
Forests: coniferous, 88, 90, 146-152, *162-163*; deciduous, 30, 55, 57, 59, 90-103, 114-115
Fox, gray, 101-102
Franklinia alatamaha, 56
Fraser, John, 60
French Broad River, 36
Fungi, 92; Berkeley's polypore (*Polyporus berkeleyi*), *93*; *Dactylella doedycoides*, 96; food-chain role, 90-91; ganoderma, *75*; hyphae, 91-92; lycogala epidendrum slime mold, *95*; mychorhizial relationships, 92; witch's butter jelly (*Guepinia spathulata*), *95*. *See also* Lichen(s); Mushrooms

G

Gneiss, *136-137*; arkose, 78; striated, *142*
Grahame, Kenneth, 87
Grand Caverns (Virginia), 154
Grandfather Mountain, 24, 57

Grass(es): bald oat (*Danthonia compressus*), *160*; bent (*Agrostis perrenans*), *160*; panic, 78
Great Smoky Mountains, *12-13*, 22, 27, 28-29, 34, *58*, *59*; winter in, *166-179*. See also Plott Balsam Mountains.
Great Smoky Mountains National Park, *52-53*, 62, 101, 104, 114, *115*, 123, 154
Greenbrier, 65
Greenbrier Cove, 63

H
Hawksbill Mountain, 83
Heaths, 31, 51. See also Balds, heath
Hemlock(s) (*Tsuga canadensis*), 72-73, *74-75*, 84
Hobble: dog (*Leucothoë editorum*), 38, *46*; witch (*Viburnum alnifolium*), *48-49*
Honeysuckle, trumpet (*Lonicera sempervirens*), 38, *41*
Horse sugar, or sweetleaf (*Symplocus tinctoria*), 79
Huckleberry, 51, *112*
Humus, 90, 97

I
Indian paintbrush (*Castilleja coccinea*), *40*
Indian plantain, Rugel's (*Cacalia rugelia*), *66-67*
Indians, 153; aboriginal population, 60, 153; Apalachee, 21; Cherokee, 54, 55, 60
Insects: aquatic, 129, 130; caddis flies, 129; centipedes, 86, 99; comma butterfly, 27; hunting spider, 98; millipedes, 77, 86, 97; pill bug, 86, 97; species survival, 98-99; walkingstick, 24-25; water strider, 80, *81*. See also Beetles
Iris, crested dwarf (*Iris cristata*), 38, *41*, 79

J
Jefferson, Thomas, 152; quoted, 20

L
Lady's-slipper, pink (*Cypripedum acaule*), *41*
Laurel(s), 38, 82; mountain (*Kalmia latifolia*), 31, *51*
Le Conte, Mount, 27, 31, *167*
Lichen(s), *75*, 149-150, 165; rock tripe (*Umbilicaria mammylata*), 75-76
Linville Falls, end paper 3-page 1, 72, 73
Linville Gorge (Pisgah National Forest), 72-85
Linville River, 72, *76-77*, 80
Little Pigeon River, *172*; West Prong, 30, 132
Little River, *118-119*; the Sinks, 116-133, 165
Liverworts, 82, *83*
Logging, *60-61*, 62
Luray Caverns (Virginia), *156-157*

M
McCurdy, John Chang, 166
Magnolia(s), 59, 63; *Magnolia auriculata*, 55; umbrella (*Magnolia tripetala*), *48*
Maple(s), 30, 38, 63, 64
May apple (*Podophyllum peltatum*), *48*
Mayfly, 129
Medsger, Oliver P., quoted, 75-76
Michaux, André, 59-60
Minerals: alum salts, 31; limestone cave formations, *155*, *156-157*
Mitchell, Elisha, 148
Mitchell, Mount (North Carolina), 23, 24, *32-33*; forest, 147-150, 152; logging on, *60-61*; State Park, 22
Monongahela National Forest, *4-5*, *151*, 158, 161
Moss(es), 82, *83*, 147, 150; sphagnum, 159, 161, 164
Mountain-folding, *28-29*
Mountain ash, 37, 62
Mushrooms, 91; brick-top (*Hypholoma sublateritium fries*), *93*; broad-gilled collybia (*Collybia platyphylla fries*), *95*; Caesar's (*Amanita hemibafa*), *93*; chanterelle hygrophorus (*Hygrophorus cantharellus*), *94*; chicken (*Polyporus sulphureus*), *95*; Coker's amanita (*Amanita cokeri gilbert*), *94*; destroying angel, 91; jack o'lantern (*Omphalotus olearius*), *94*; lepiota, *94*; reticulate-stemmed bolete (*Boletus retipes berkeley & curtis*), *94*
Myrtle(s), 31, 38; mountain (*Leiophyllum lyoni*), 51, *84*

N
Nantahala Mountains, 54, 68
National Park Service, 34, 104
Nematodes, 96, 97
Newfound Gap, 62, *176*

O
Oak(s), *23*, 38, 55, 63, 84
Onion Mountain (North Carolina), end paper 1
Orchids: purple fringed (*Habenaria psycodes*), 38, *43*; showy orchis, (*Orchis spectabilis*), 82, *83*

P
Peattie, Donald Culross, quoted, 63-64, 116
Peattie, Roderick, quoted, 86
Phacelia, white-fringed (*Phacelia fimbriata*), *46*
Phlox, trailing (*Phlox stolonifera*), *46-47*
Pisgah National Forest, 70, 98
Platt, Rutherford, quoted, 149
Plott Balsam Mountains, 25
Protozoa, food-chain role of, 96

R
Rafinesque-Schmaltz, Constantine Samuel, 60
Ragwort: golden (*Senecio aurens*), *40*; Rugel's, 34
Rainbow's Arc (Fighting Creek), *177*
Redbud(s) (*Cercis canadensis*), 38, *39*
Rhododendron(s), end papers 1-2, 31, 38, 51, 65, 73, 81, 82, 84, *170-171*; catawba (*Rhododendron catawbiense*), *52-53*; rosebay, 30
Roan Mountain, 24
Rock formations, *78*; Babel Tower Rock, 79; gorges, 72; graybacks, 65; metamorphic, 78, 79. See also Gneiss
Russell Fork River, *6-7*

S
Salamanders, 36-37, 80, 87; Blue Ridge Mountain (*Desmognathus*

ochrophaeus carolinensis), 35; hellbender, or water dog, 132-133; marbled *(Ambystoma opacum), 35;* red-cheeked *(Plethodon jordani jordani), 35, 37;* spotted *(Ambystoma maculatum), 35*
Sassafras, 79
Saxifrage, 149
Sedge, *4-5*
Sentell, Rex, 118, 127
Shady Valley (Tennessee), 159, 161, 165
Sharp, Aaron J., 46
Shenandoah National Park, 158
Shrews, 99-100
Silver bell(s) *(Halesia carolina), 12, 48,* 64, 82
Skunks, 101
Skyline Caverns (Virginia), *154*
Smith, C. W., 84
Smoky Mountains, or Smokies. See Great Smoky Mountains
Snails, 97; polygrid, *77*
Snakes, 87, 99; coral *(Micrurus fulvius fulvius),* 99, *100;* mole, 87; rat, 25, 99; ring-necked, 37; scarlet *(Cemophora coccinea),* 99, *100;* scarlet king *(Lampropeltis elapsoides elapsoides),* 99, *100*
Solomon's-seal *(Polygonatum biflorum),* 41, 44
Southern Appalachians, *2-3, 18-19,* 20, 21, 27, 31, 34, *174-175;* annual precipitation, 26-27; geology and extent, 21-23; ice age, 34, 36, 57, 59; park systems, 22, 24; peaks, 24; species variety, 34, 36, 38, 114. See *also* Allegheny Mountains; Blue Ridge Mountains
Spence Field, *160*
Spiderwort *(Tradescantia virginiana),* 41, *42*
Spotswood, Sir Alexander, 154
Springtails, food-chain role, 96-97
Spruce, red *(Picea rubens),* 26, *88-89,* 147-148, *162-163*
Squirrels, 68; flying, 68, 70; gray, 68; red *(Tamiasciurus hudsonicus), 69*
Stonefly, *126,* 129
Stupka, Arthur, 70
Sweet gums, 55, 57

T
Tablerock Mountain, 83
Tennessee River, 117, 125
Toad, American, 98
Todd, James, 154
Touch-me-not, or jewelweed, 80, *81*
Trillium, painted *(Trillium undulatum), 72, 73*
Trout, 121, 122; brook *(Salvelinus fontinalis),* 122, *123;* brown, 117, 121, 122, 126; color changing, 124; hatchery vs. native, 126; rainbow *(Salmo gairdneri irideus),* 117, 120, *123;* sense perception, 120-121; territorial instinct, 125-126
Tulip tree(s), *12,* 55, 57, 59, 63, 64, 70-71, 83-84, 165
Turtlehead, purple, 149

U
Umbrella leaf *(Diphylleia cymosa), 48*
University of Tennessee, 104, 111

V
Valley Head (West Virginia), 154
Vegetation, 30-31, 36, 37; and auxin, 66; bog, 159, 161, 164; emigrant, 41; endangered, 41; endemic, 34, 41, 46, 52, *66-67;* food-chain role, 90-103; heath bald, 31; immigrant, 41; nurse logs and, 31; variety, 38, 55, 59, 91. See *also specific types;* Forests
Violets, 80, *81;* Canada *(Viola canadensis), 43*
Voles *(Microtus pennsylvanicus), 96,* 100

W
Walch, Robert, 72
Waterfall, *82-83*
Weather: annual precipitation, 26-27, 73; hoarfrost, *32-33, 166, 167;* seasonal changes, 166-179
Whaley, Zenith, 63, 64, 65, 66, 70, 71
Wild and Scenic Rivers Act (1968), 134
Wiseman's View, 83, *84-85*
Wood sorrel *(Oxalis montana),* 41, *43,* 149
Wordsworth, William, quoted, 59

Printed in U.S.A.